Windows For Sermons

Stories And Humor For Inspired Preaching

Don R. Yocom

CSS Publishing Company, Inc., Lima, Ohio

WINDOWS FOR SERMONS

Copyright © 2000 by
CSS Publishing Company, Inc.
Lima, Ohio

Some scripture quotations are from the *King James Version of the Bible*, in the public
domain.

Some scripture quotations are from the *Holy Bible, New International Version*, Copyright
© 1973, 1978, 1984 International Bible Society. Used by permission of Zondervan Bible
Publishers. All rights reserved.

Library of Congress Cataloging-in-Publication Data

Yocom, Don R.
   Windows for sermons: stories and humor for inspired preaching/Don R. Yocom.
     p.   cm.
   ISBN 0-7880-1570-2 (pbk. : acid-free paper)
   1. Homiletical illustrations. I. Title.
BV4225.2.Y63 2000
251'.08—dc21   99-054634
                                                 CIP

This book is available in the following formats, listed by ISBN:
    0-7880-1570-2   Book
    0-7880-1571-0   Disk
    0-7880-1572-9   Sermon Prep

PRINTED IN U.S.A.

To "Dottie,"
my wife and co-worker in ministry
for over fifty years

Topical Index

Introduction

Jesus was a master story teller who used many appropriate illustrations as windows for his messages. What samples we have in the Gospels give us insight into why his three years of ministry were so effective.

Good pastors are always looking for striking illustrations for their sermons. Such an illustration can be like a window to give light and understanding to the main topic at hand.

During more than fifty years in the ministry I have gathered and used these amazing stories to help the listeners get the point more readily. And listeners have informed me that they have been awakened to response by the various illustrations given.

For example, I remember the effect the story of "The Man In An Old Corduroy Coat" had on a youth rally of some 800 youth in Springfield, Ohio. Many were challenged never to throw out of their lives the one who could save them. Many can still tell where they heard the story and who related it that night, more than thirty years ago.

We find "windows for sermons" in the newspaper comics. They may be from Charlie Brown or in the *Family Circus*, or even in *B.C.* Also, a radio announcer gave us the story, "Did Hell Freeze Over?"

The Bible is full of meaningful illustrations, so we have included some of them here. The daily news also contributes stories we can use, if we will listen and apply the truth. Personal experiences related well also.

Let us brighten up our sermons, so that their message will not be forgotten. These illustrations are presented for that purpose.

Don R. Yocom

1. That Remarkable Drinking Fountain

On a hot Summer day a minister paused in a town plaza to get a drink of water. There was a fountain near the garden wall, so he waited as a boy ahead of him had a drink.

When his time came the minister reached for a lever or button and could find none! He looked around to see if there was a foot control, but no, there was no such thing. How do I get a drink, he mused.

It didn't bother the lad ahead of him. He just bowed his head and drank the water. That must be it!

So the minister bowed his head over the fountain and the water came. He realized then that the fountain was controlled by a hidden ray that he caused to work by bowing his head.

What a striking example of faith that boy had demonstrated to the minister by bowing his head.

2. The Man In An Old Corduroy Coat

The telephone rang in a noted surgeon's home on the outskirts of a large city. It was in the wee hours of the morning. When the surgeon answered it, he heard the voice of a staff doctor at the hospital where he worked calling him to come immediately. A child was violently ill and the only answer was surgery. Of course he would come.

Quickly he dressed, grabbed his doctor's case, and drove toward the city. At the first traffic light at the bare edge of town he had to stop because it signaled red. Then it happened: the door of the car on the passenger side opened and a man entered and seated himself. He was dressed in an old brown corduroy coat with a shabby brown cap on his head.

When the light changed, the surgeon started again only to have a gun poked in his ribs and the passenger said, "Stop the car!" What could the doctor do? He stopped, and when the man said,

"Get out!" what else could he do with a gun in his ribs! He got out; the man took over the car and sped away.

The surgeon walked with his doctor's case to the nearest gasoline station quite a distance ahead, very upset over what had happened. There he called a taxi which was slow arriving. Eventually he got to the hospital. A lot of time had elapsed.

"Too late!" they told him in surgery; the child had died. If only he had been there in time ...

Then the inevitable and difficult question: "Would you talk with the child's family?" He consented, wondering what to say.

When he entered the room, in it there was only one person: the man in the brown corduroy coat with a shabby brown cap in his hand! That man had forced out of his life the only person who could have saved his child's life!

(A true story written originally by Billy Rose in a newspaper column many years ago.)

3. T. L. C. (Tender Loving Care)

There came one night to a little hotel desk in a busy city, a middle aged couple. The lady was tired and ill. They had hunted all over and had found no place to sleep. When the young hotel manager realized their need, he told the man:"I don't have a room left, but I am sorry about your wife. I am young and would not miss it. Take my room and rest, and everything will be all right."

The next morning the guest asked to see the young manager. In the office he produced his business card and gave it to the young man.

"My name is Astor, John Jacob Astor. I am from New York City. You are the best hotel man I have ever met. If you will allow me to do it, I will build for you the greatest hotel ever erected in the United States."

For years that young fellow, George C. Boldt, was the manager of the great Waldorf Astoria Hotel in New York City. He had practiced Tender Loving Care.

4. The Power Of A Name

The name Cadbury in England is as well known there as Hershey is in America, or Nestle in Switzerland. All three are chocolate manufacturers. The Cadbury family has been part of the Society of Friends, Quakers, for many years — very devout and generous. They have amassed a great fortune.

After World War I a large department store in London wanted to expand, but the Quaker Meetinghouse next door was in their way. They sent a letter to the religious body, offering to buy the property for a good price.

In due season the department store office received this terse reply:

QUAKER MEETINGHOUSE

We were here before you. We will not sell. (Signed) CADBURY

The store had to make other plans. Oh, the power of a name! See Philippians 2:10-11.

5. Throw An Old Ram Over The Fence!

Years ago a kindly old Scottish Presbyterian minister, who was remembered only as "Dr. McArthur," used to visit colleges where students were preparing for the ministry. Dr. McArthur's daughter-in-law was Helen Hayes (McArthur), a famous Broadway actress and a noted Christian.

The good old Scotsman would gather us young theologs together and give us wise counsel for our coming years. We could ask him questions and he often had a humorous answer.

Someone asked him about what to do with a cantankerous layman. Dr. McArthur, with a twinkle in his eye, said: "Pastors are supposed to be shepherds of the sheep. And most of the sheep will follow your leadership. But once in a while you may have to throw an old ram over the fence!"

Prophetic words, indeed!

6. So Help Me God

George Washington, America's first president, has been called by various descriptions, like "The Father of Our Country." History has recorded the kind of leadership he gave the Continental Army in the struggle for freedom. From Valley Forge to Yorktown he was the commander-in-Chief, establishing a standard seldom met by those who followed him in service to their country.

Of course, he was a great private citizen, and an outstanding jurist before he was called into service for the new country in the making. Washington was a member and an elder of the Episcopal Church, just a step off the Anglican Church, in America. In his public statements he spoke of God in a way that demonstrated his faith in the Lord as one who would help humankind in time of need. It was only right that fellow Americans would call upon him to be the first President of the United States of America.

The day of inauguration came, and time came for George to take the oath of office and make his pledge to lead. After he spoke his vows, he added four more words never before used that way. He said: **So help me God!**

The humility of this great man was so impressive, his addition of those four words set a precedent to their use almost universally as other citizens have spoken vows before man and God. Can we do less?

7. If Only A Picture Of Jesus Can Do That!

A Christian youth and three non-Christian friends were walking on Charles Street in Baltimore, Maryland, during the 1940s. When they came to what was then the Cokesbury Book Store, the Christian said, "I'm going in here to get a gift for my girlfriend's birthday." They all entered, looked around, and finally the gift was chosen. It was an 8" x 10" copy of Warner Sallman's *Head Of Christ* painting.

After leaving the store another of the guys said, "Okay, we went with you into that store. Why don't we go now and get us a beer apiece?" The Christian youth decided to go along but get a soft drink instead of the beer.

The beer joint in those days was beside a drug store. Inside, the fellows were seated at a table and the waiter came to get their orders. Three of them ordered beer; the Christian youth ordered a Coke.

The waiter said, "I don't have any soft drinks, but I can go next door to the drug store and get one for you." It was okay, the guys had time. The restaurant was not busy.

While waiting, someone suggested they open the gift and look at it again. While admiring the picture of Jesus Christ, someone said, "It ought to be put up where it could be seen better than in our hands."

Looking around he saw a nail over the bar, and since the waiter had gone next door and no one was waiting at the bar, the youth went over and hung the picture of Christ on the nail. It was amazing what effect it had on the place!

The waiter returned and sensed what had happened when he saw the picture. He took it down and gave it to the Christian youth and said, "Religion and this business don't mix!"

The fellows finished their drinks and went outside. One of them spoke up: "If only a picture of Jesus can do that, what would actually knowing him be like?" The Christian answered and eventually led the three of them to accept Christ as their Savior.

8. Keep Your Fork!

We go to a banquet and enjoy it very much. There are many pleasant words exchanged, and the food is good. There comes a lull when the waitress takes our plate and advises, "Keep your fork!"

Now you and I know what that means. Sure!

There's something more for us as we look forward to the dessert, and we hope it is even better than the first part of the meal. It usually is.

That's the way with eternal life. When we die physically we hope for something better in the next life.

Keep your fork! Yes, and enjoy what God has for his believers in eternity.

9. The Little Red Wagon Story

After the bombing of Pearl Harbor and our entrance into World War II, the U.S. Government decided to build the Pentagon. This was to become the largest building in America; it has five stories down as well as up. A call was issued by newspapers and radio that trucks would be needed to haul away the dirt from the large excavation.

A ten-year-old boy with a little red wagon showed up at headquarters to help move the dirt. He was turned away by the man in charge of the early shift. He was also turned away by the man in charge of the next shift. But when the boy, in tears, turned to leave, the Army General in charge of the entire project overheard the conversation and spoke to the lad.

"Why is it so important to you to get a job working with your little red wagon on this building?"

The boy answered, "I saw in the paper that we needed this building because we were not prepared. I lost my daddy at Pearl Harbor because of that. I thought if I could help just a little we might get this building done sooner, and some other boy might not lose his daddy."

The big-hearted General gave orders, "Give this boy a number." They pinned a truck number on his T-shirt. "Take his wagon over to the shop and paint a number on it." It was done. The boy went to work.

Later, observers noted the boy moving small piles of dirt. It would have taken a million years to move the amount that had to be moved so that the building could be built.

But, when the other workmen heard *why* the boy was there they moved heaven and earth to get the job done. It had an all time record for the completion of such a huge project. Much of it because a ten-year-old boy said, "All I have to give my country is myself and my red wagon."

All that any of us have to give is our talent of service for God and country.

(Story recorded in *Bits And Pieces*, by O. B. Spencer, Providence House Publishers, Franklin, Tennessee. Used by permission.)

10. Did Hell Freeze Over?

A popular announcer told the story on a radio broadcast about a little girl who told her parents she wanted a bunny rabbit for her birthday. Her father said, "Hell will have to freeze over before I will let you have a rabbit."

But the child was optimistic about it all. When cold weather came she would ask every morning if it was cold enough for Hell to freeze over. Her mother told her not to expect too much.

But one morning the child heard a weather broadcaster on a Detroit, Michigan, radio station tell how cold it had been the night before. He said, "Hell froze over last night!"

The little girl was ecstatic, and ran to tell her father what had been announced on the radio report. "Hell froze over last night!"

The child got her rabbit the next day.

(Hell is the name of a town in Michigan.)

11. Who Was Jemima? Who Was Her Father?

Invariably, if you ask this question, even in a Bible study class, you will get smiles, and someone will say, "You mean Aunt Jemima?"

The "Jemima" named in the *NIV* translation of the Bible was the first named of three daughters and seven sons of a very well known citizen of the land of Uz. The *NIV* indicates that she was beautiful.

Bible scholars say her father lived in that period between the writings of Samuel and Isaiah. It is generally agreed he was an Israelite.

There were some other attractive women mentioned in Bible times, including Rebekah and Rachel.

Who was Jemima's father? Job (Job 42:14).

12. The Cross In A Man's Pocket

When Don Rummel opened his welding and repair shop in Wapakoneta, Ohio, in the 1960s, God led him to start an unusual form of evangelism. He laid out on the counter beside the cash register a box that all customers could see. It was filled with small aluminum crosses. A sign above, pointing to the box, read: FREE. There was also a pile of cards in the box on which was printed the poem, "The Cross In My Pocket."

Customers of all kinds came to the welding shop. There were farmers with plowshares to mend, and men who work with heavy machinery like backhoes and power shovels. Some were tough-looking guys.

It has been interesting to know that when some of the men saw the FREE sign they checked on it and often picked up one of the bits of aluminum, two inches long, on which was printed: GOD LOVES YOU. Then the poem was scrutinized. Only if they asked Don, or his son Douglas, would they have any questions answered.

Often men would just stuff a cross and a card in their pockets, as if to say, "I'll look at this later."

Yes, it has done a lot of good, as some customers later told Don. But he never knew in this world all of the good that has come from giving many men a cross on which is printed the essence of the gospel of Christ.

Now he knows. Don went to be with his Lord in 1996.

```
          L
    G  O  D
          V
          E
          S
          *
          Y
          O
          U
```

13. The Backhoe Operator

You may have seen a backhoe in operation. It is a form of the power scoopshovel which works in the opposite direction, to dig out a trench or clean out a ditch.

A member of our rural church operated a backhoe for a living. When asked if he liked his work, he surprised me.

"Yes, I do," he replied. "I take the machinery to the place needing it and begin working. It may be a drainage ditch I am to open. When I start, the ditch is a mess, clogged up with debris and stagnant water."

He continued, "It is a joy for me to see what happens when the ditch is cleared of its rubble. The water starts to flow again, and soon it is all clear. The drainage can go as it should. The work with the backhoe has made it possible, and I am satisfied."

What an illustration that is of the cleansing power of the Holy Spirit, who can remove the obstacles that hindered God's power to flow into our souls.

14. Can The Master Use Your Instrument?

The young organist in a European city church became aware that there was a visitor in the church sanctuary that afternoon. At a break in the music, the visitor came to the organ bench and asked if he might play the organ.

The young man was disturbed, for he felt that it was an intrusion into his personal time and the use of the fine instrument before him. Finally, he reluctantly gave in and the man moved to the organ bench.

It wasn't long before the young organist realized that the visitor was a great musician. The organ gave forth such wonderful music, it made quite an impression on him. How wrong he had been!

Too soon the rendition of a fine composition ended and the visitor stepped away from the organ bench. He thanked the young organist for granting permission for him to play the organ, then started to leave. The young man did get his wits together enough to ask the man's name.

"My name? My name is Felix Mendelssohn," he said. Then he left the sanctuary.

The experience touched the young man's soul. His comment then, and later when he related the event to others, was, "And to think, I almost did not let the master use my instrument!"

How many of us today, looking back on events in our lives, could say the same thing:

"I almost did not let the Master use my instrument!"

15. Who Was George Ames?

A true pioneer of world missions was Adoniram Judson. His life story had an amazing incident worth telling.

A brilliant student, when Adoniram was twelve years old he was capable of teaching the Bible in its original languages. He was such a gifted student in college he began to think of himself more highly than he should. He became quite an agnostic.

Judson drew other students to him. Among those who became atheists was one named George Ames who became quite a spokesman for that point of view.

Some years passed. Travel was hard in those days, and after an exhausting day Judson wearily inquired at a hotel for a room. All the rooms were taken except one next to the room in which a dying man was raving in his delirium.

Judson took the room, but at first slept very little as he kept hearing the vile language of the dying man. Later he did go to sleep. The next morning when preparing to leave the hotel he told the attendant of his experience. The man in the next room had died during the night. When Adoniram Judson asked the man's name the attendant said, "George Ames." The name stirred the soul of Judson, because Ames had been one of those students who had learned all about atheism some years before!

As Judson traveled that morning, the impact of what he had heard that night so affected him that he knelt by the dusty road and prayed to God the prayer of repentance.

God not only heard his prayer, but sent Adoniram Judson as a missionary to Asia. His mission in Burma was so difficult he labored seven years before he had one convert. Tested in those years by the loss of his wife, and by being sent to prison for teaching what was a new way of life for the Burmese, life was hard for Judson. But he never forgot George Ames and what it means to be lost.

16. Warner Sallman's *Head Of Christ*

Dr. Charles R. Goff, the pastor of Chicago Temple Methodist Church in post-World War I days, was lecturing at a Chicago YMCA. He titled his address: "What I think Jesus was like."

The pastor deplored the fact that so many artists' paintings of the years past made Jesus appear pale and with a meek personality. Of course, we know Jesus did suffer on the cross, but Dr. Goff thought Jesus had strong features worth describing. So he told the audience what he thought Jesus might have looked like. He gave a word for word striking description of Jesus.

In an adjoining room, a young unknown artist overheard the pastor's lecture. He was so affected by it that he set out to paint the *Head of Christ* as Dr. Goff gave his version. The artist was Warner Sallman.

The painting was slow being accepted, at first, because it showed striking features with positive lines, high cheek bones, olive colored skin, and powerful eyes that command attention. This was so different.

It finally appeared on a magazine cover, and people began to ask questions about this new concept in the painting of Christ, so different from the stereotypes of the past.

From there the popularity began. Today it can easily be said that no other painting has had such universal appeal. More copies of this painting have been sold than of any other religious painting, and it is still a best seller.

(I heard Dr. Goff tell this true story years ago at a pastor's meeting.)

17. He Got His Hat Back

A pastor decided to go on a vacation on short notice. He called a retired pastor to fill the pulpit while he was gone. He said the visiting pastor could have the offering that Sunday. But when the visiting pastor announced at the service that they would be taking a special offering for him, the congregation had not been informed it was supposed to happen.

The ushers were called. They took the offering plates to the pews, then returned with them to the front of the church. It was obvious that the people were not prepared for it and no offerings were in the plates.

Thinking that if he had the ushers pass his hat, the people might be generous, he sent the ushers back to pass the hat and then bring it forward. This they did.

The pastor looked in the hat, saw nothing, turned the hat over and shook it. Nothing fell out. Then he prayed, "I am thankful, Lord, that I got my hat back from this congregation!"

18. I'd Rather Have Jesus Than Silver Or Gold

In the years of the Great Depression in America, the 1930s, a popular network radio program was "Hymns of All Nations," originating in Chicago, Illinois. Joe Emerson, the soloist, suffered a heart attack and a substitute had to be found on short notice. A rather unknown musician was asked to fill in. He had come up with a new hymn that he sang on the broadcast, and it won public acclaim. The hymn was titled, "I'd Rather Have Jesus Than Silver Or Gold." The singer was George Beverly Shea.

In the meantime, the Reverend Billy Graham was becoming quite well-known as an evangelist, and a relationship was soon established between the two men. In keeping with evangelistic tradition of Moody and Sankey, Billy Sunday and Homer Rodeheaver, it was inevitable that Billy Graham and "Bev" Shea work together. This team, with Cliff Barrows, has been together for fifty years and is well known throughout Christendom.

Bev Shea's mother had given him the poem; he wrote the music for it. It has been used around the world. It speaks well of a man whose dedication to Christ has been recognized universally.

19. The Great Stone Face

A boy named Ernest, who grew up within sight of this famous mountain near Franconia Notch, New Hampshire, had heard the community legend that some day a man would come to the town who would look like that great stone face.

Ernest set his goal in life to find that man.

Years passed and though he sought far and wide, in his old age Ernest despaired that the legend would come true. When he expressed his thoughts to friends about it, they informed Ernest that *he* was that very man! He actually looked like the great stone face.

The moral of the story:

The thing we seek for in life is what we become.

(Read Nathaniel Hawthorne's classic story of "The Great Stone Face.")

20. Ode To Joy

Ludwig van Beethoven was one of the truly great musicians of all time. His music appeals to us even today, long after it was written. Possibly his greatest composition was his "Ode To Joy" from his celebrated *Ninth Symphony*. We hear this music often in both secular and religious realms.

For example, "Ode To Joy" was used at the recent Olympic Games. It is often used at state occasions. It is so easy to enjoy and remember.

In the church hymnal we find it with the words, "Joyful, Joyful, We Adore Thee." These choice words were added to the music by the well-known author of a century ago, Henry Van Dyke.

The striking thing about all this is that Beethoven *never* actually *heard* the music he had written. He was deaf! But the tune sang its way into his heart as it does ours. Of such is true greatness composed.

21. Recycling The Universe

The idea of recycling metal cans, plastic milk bottles, and newspapers has saved us all money and has proved to be a more efficient stewardship of the basic materials in the environment.

But the striking fact is that this is not a twentieth century idea at all. God established our universe with a huge recycling system from the beginning of time! It has long been an established truth that humankind cannot make any new elements of basic matter, nor completely destroy them. What we have done has been to deliberately misuse the elements and make them unfit for our greedy materialistic society now and possibly for many years to come.

We should be good Christian stewards of all we have been given by a wise God, whose natural world practices recycling far better than does mankind. This might be called the long range redemption of our physical world, but God has plenty of time!

22. A Cup Of Coffee And A Piece Of Toast

How an afternoon snack led to building a Senior Retirement Center in a town of 8,000 people.

When the pastor called, Martha Kiggins, a shut-in, was finishing an afternoon snack of a cup of coffee and a piece of toast. It was a Wednesday afternoon in 1961. He asked her when was the last time she had eaten a good full-sized meal.

She thought a bit, then answered, "My nephew brought me a fine dinner on Sunday noon." Sunday to Wednesday! She said she wasn't hungry most of that time, so just had a piece of toast now and then. She looked like she needed nourishment.

The pastor wondered how many other shut-ins were like that. He made a study of the town and wrote letters to the editor of the town newspaper, who supported the idea. They needed a place for Senior Citizens to receive good care at reasonable rates.

Then came a pleasant surprise. An eccentric retired stock broker, Mr. Arnold Dienstberger, offered a trust account worth over

82,000 dollars in memory of his wife — if the town would match the gift. The churches and schools began to work on the project. The community supported it and raised over 90,000 dollars. Today there are facilities for 100 people readily available for people like Miss Kiggins who obviously had needed such care.

Notice these ecumenical facts:

* The stock broker was Lutheran.
* The pastor was a United Methodist (so was Martha Kiggins).
* The editor of the newspaper was a Jew.
* The co-chairman in the developing organization was a Roman Catholic priest.
* All churches in the town participated including United Methodist, Lutheran, Roman Catholic, Presbyterian, Christian Union, Assembly of God, the Church of the Nazarene, and the Evangelical United Brethren.

The name of the town — Delphos, Ohio.

The Care Center — Van Crest of Delphos.

23. That Sinking Feeling

At dusk, a delivery truck driver was on a lonely road in Eastern Indiana when it appeared to him that there was a wall two feet high directly across the road in front of him. Perplexed, he stopped and looked farther only to see the wall was gradually rising! No, he was sinking!

The man got out of his truck and realized the road was sinking into a peat bog over which it had been built years before. Peat was oozing up on each side of the road. He ran back to what appeared to be a safe distance. Looking back in the waning light he thought the sinking had stopped. He walked quickly to a nearby farmhouse and placed a phone call for help. The wrecker got his truck out before a stretch of 300 feet of roadway sunk below the oozing peat.

It happened near Matthews, Grant County, Indiana, in the 1930s. What a scary experience it would be to have what one thought was so dependable and safe disappear under one's feet! (See 1 Corinthians 10:12.)

24. Mount Rushmore

It is a great sight to see for the first time the faces of four presidents of our country carved into the side of Mount Rushmore in the Black Hills of South Dakota. The faces include George Washington, Abraham Lincoln, Thomas Jefferson, and Theodore Roosevelt.

The features are so vast that those workmen doing the carving would often be uncertain what to do next. Then they would go to the office building at the foot of the mountain to see, laid out in detail, the original design by the architect, Mr. Gustave Borglum.

So it is with the concept of "the Kingdom of God." When we are uncertain due to the vastness of it all, not knowing what to do next, we must look to the Holy Bible which gives us the information we need for our task in life. It tells us of others who also were on a journey of faith through God's Kingdom.

25. Bits Of Humor

We have liked the words of homespun philosophy given us by a Hoosier friend years ago. He said: "It's better to have a sense of humor than to have no sense at all!"

*   *   *   *   *

On a hot August day we saw these words on a church bulletin board:
DO YOU THINK IT'S HOT *HERE*?

*   *   *   *   *

On the walls of the Chester Cathedral in England is this bit of anonymous poetry:
>Give me a sense of humor, Lord,
>Give me the grace to see a joke,

To get some happiness in life
And pass it on to other folk.

* * * * *

It was a warm day after a rainy one, with puddles here and there. If there is anything messier than a little boy playing in a mud puddle it would be a little girl making mud pies. Her pastor came down the way, saw the child, and spoke to her.

"Betsy, you're pretty dirty, aren't you?"

The little girl stood up and said, "I'm prettier clean!"

(God's redeeming power can take the dirtiest people and make them clean.)

* * * * *

Seen on a T-shirt!

"Please be patient. God isn't through with me yet."

* * * * *

The Sunday School teacher was talking to children about loving God with all your heart. She asked them a question:"Where is your heart?"

All of the children but one put their hands on their chest. That one child put her hand on her back side. The teacher wanted to know why.

"When Grandma comes," the child said, "she pats me back there and says, 'Bless your little heart.' "

* * * * *

Drive carefully. Heaven can wait!

* * * * *

30

The philosophy of the sweet potato: I YAM WHAT I YAM.

* * * * *

On grace before meals, a preacher asked a lad, "Boy, tell me, do you at your house have prayer before meals?"
Lad: "No, my mom's a good cook!"

* * * * *

Did you hear the joke about the cookie?
"No, tell me."
"Okay. It's crumby."

* * * * *

After a man told his little son about Noah and the ark, the boy asked, "Hey, Dad, why didn't Noah swat those two flies?"

* * * * *

Matrimony is the splice of life.

* * * * *

It was time to read the pastor's appointments at West Ohio Annual Conference of the Methodist Episcopal Church, time about the 1920s. Rev. Henry Cooper had served most of his years in west and northwest Ohio. The bishop read, "Catawba — Rev. Henry Cooper." There was silence. Then the voice of Henry, "My God, Bishop, where is Catawba?" The congregation burst out with laughter.

* * * * *

It was a hot, humid afternoon wedding. The bridegroom had a time trying to slide the wedding ring on the bride's finger. Seated where she could see everything, the groom's aunt in a loud but hoarse whisper said, "Spit on it, John!"

31

* * * * *

"I can't sleep!" the preacher's wife told him. "Preach me one of your sermons!"
(reported by Bishop Tutu of South Africa)

* * * * *

How should we pronounce "Appalachia?" Some say it should be said like in the story of Eve leaving the Garden of Eden. She was confronted by the serpent, and is reported to have said: "Get out of my way, Satan, or I'll throw my Appalachia!"

* * * * *

Seen on a church bulletin board:
"Come early for a good back seat!"

* * * * *

A Quaker was reported to have bought a cow with a bad disposition. Sometimes it would kick whoever tried to milk it, or at least upset the bucket.

After one difficult milking time, when the cow both kicked the Quaker and his milk bucket, the Quaker walked around in front of the animal and said: "Cow, thou knowest that I am a peace-loving Quaker. I do not believe in punishing thee for kicking me. But what thou dost not know is that I could sell thee to a Methodist!"

* * * * *

When down in the mouth remember Jonah. He came out all right!

* * * * *

When asked about a picture of some angry mules in his study, the retired pastor said, "That's a picture of my last Official Board!"

* * * * *

Children in a Sunday School class were instructed to write a Bible verse about missions that they could remember. One youngster wrote: "Go into all the world and spread the gossip."

* * * * *

Two dogs watched a couple dance the disco. After a while one turned to the other and said, "If we did that they'd worm us!"

* * * * *

Don't worry if your job is small,
And your rewards are few;
Remember that the mighty oak
Was once a nut like you!
— Anonymous

* * * * *

Noted for his great sense of humor, Bishop Edwin H. Hughes was about to read the pastor's appointments at a North Indiana Conference of the Methodist Episcopal Church. It was during pre-World War II days.

The large church was packed with intense listeners. Just then, an older man on a front seat gave out a roof-raising sneeze.

The bishop paused, then looking down over his glasses, said, "These appointments are nothing to be sneezed at!"

The congregation roared with laughter.

* * * * *

Another who had a great sense of humor was Dr. Samuel F. Upham of Drew Theological Seminary, Madison, New Jersey. At his deathbed friends and relatives had gathered. Dr. Upham had been an authority on the lives of church martyrs.

The question arose whether Dr. Upham was still living or not. Someone advised, "Feel his feet. No one ever died with warm feet."

Dr. Upham opened one eye and said, "John Hus did!" Then Upham died!

* * * * *

There is so much good in the worst of us,
And so much bad in the best of us,
That it hardly becomes any of us
To talk about the rest of us.
— Anonymous

* * * * *

A lively Senior Citizen was celebrating his 104th birthday. He was interviewed by a newspaper reporter who asked this question: "Sir, to what do you attribute your being able to live so long and still be quite well?"

The Senior Citizen answered, "Well now, I have been taking vitamins and minerals ever since I was 100 years old."

* * * * *

Our fathers have been churchmen
Nineteen hundred years or so;
And to every new proposal,
They have always answered "No!"
— Anonymous

* * * * *

They tell this one in the hill country of southern Ohio. There was an odd character by the name of Joshua. He had to go to court where the judge asked him, "Are you the Joshua who made the sun stand still?" (Joshua 10:12-13).

His answer was, "No, I'm the Joshua that made the moonshine."

* * * * *

The seminary student walked his date to her dormitory on the adjacent college campus, and felt like he wanted to kiss her goodnight. But he had asked his Bible professor about Romans 16:16: "Greet one another with a holy kiss," only to be told the passage referred to the greeting in a worship service.

When they arrived at the dorm the girl turned and kissed him! Surprise! He asked if she could give him a biblical approval for it, and she quoted: "Do unto others as you would have them do unto you" (Matthew 7:12).

* * * * *

Gossips have a great sense of rumor.

* * * * *

College Humor:

At the dining hall of Asbury College, Wilmore, Kentucky, there was a large bowl of nice red apples with this notice:

TAKE ONLY ONE, GOD IS WATCHING

At the other end of the food line there was a bin of leftover broken cookies. Some student had scrawled on a piece of notebook paper a notice:

TAKE ALL YOU WANT, GOD IS WATCHING THE APPLES

* * * * *

A little school boy was heard reciting the pledge of allegiance to the flag as follows: "I pledge my allowance to the flag of the United States of America."

* * * * *

A little girl asked her mother if the television comedian Red Skelton would go to heaven when he died. She really liked him.

Mother: "Well, I think he will."

Child: "Oh, Momma, won't God laugh?"

*   *   *   *   *

Children's Variations of "The Lord's Prayer":

Our Father, who art in Heaven, Harold be Thy Name.

Or

Our Father, who art in Heaven, Halloween Thy Name.

Lead us not into Penn Station.

Give us this day our jelly bread.

Forgive us our trash baskets as we forgive others their trash baskets.

*   *   *   *   *

On a church bulletin board:

TRY OUR SUNDAY SPECIAL — SOUL FOOD

*   *   *   *   *

A teenage boy was watching television when the phone rang. It was his dad.

"Where's your mother?" he asked.

The boy said, "She's out working in the garden."

Dad barked on the phone, "What? Your mother is not as young and strong as she used to be. Why aren't you out there helping her?"

The reply was: "I can't. Grandma is using the other hoe!"

*   *   *   *   *

Seen on a T-shirt:

I'M O.K. GOD DOESN'T MAKE JUNK.

*   *   *   *   *

A mother heard her small daughter praying one evening. The child began slowly: "Now I lay me down to sleep." There was a pause. Then, "I pray the Lord my soul to keep." Another thoughtful pause: "If I should die before I wake." After a short wait the child excitedly repeated, "If I should die before I wake, Jesus, could we have breakfast together?"

* * * * *

Don't be angry if someone knows more than you. It's not his fault!

* * * * *

From the comic strip *Pogo*, years ago,
"We have met the enemy, and he is us."

* * * * *

On Being Healthy ...
A medical doctor and a pastor made this compact:
The pastor was to work at keeping the doctor out of Hell.
The medic was to work at keeping the pastor out of Heaven!

* * * * *

Tithing: How God's people supported the church before Bingo came along.

* * * * *

A child complained to Mommy one morning: "Mommy, I have a tummy ache, and I'm so sick."
Mommy said, "Your tummy is empty. If you will eat and put something in it, you'll feel better all over."
The child ate and then said, "I feel better."

Later that morning, the pastor called in the home. After a few remarks the mother left the room to get some coffee.

The pastor confided in the child, "I have a bad headache."

The child said, "That's because your head is empty. You'd feel better if you'd put something in it!"

* * * * *

Are you a Brylcreem Christian? Just a little dab'll do you?

* * * * *

A minister left his card at an unanswered front door, having written on it, "Revelation 3:20."

The following Sunday the woman from that house handed him a card as she left the church. On it she had written, "Genesis 3:10."

* * * * *

A tombstone is the only thing that can stand upright and lie on its face at the same time!

* * * * *

Evolution (The Monkey's Viewpoint)

Three monkeys sat in a coconut tree
Discussing things as they're said to be.
Said one to the others, "Now listen, you two,
There's a certain rumor that can't be true.
That man descended from our noble race ...
The very idea! It's a dire disgrace.
No monkey ever deserted his wife,
Starved her baby and ruined her life.
And you've never known a mother monk
To leave her babies with others to bunk,

Or, pass them on from one to another,
Till they hardly know who is their mother.
And another thing you'll never see,
A monk build a fence around a coconut tree,
And let the coconuts go to waste,
Forbidding all other monks a taste.
Why, if I put a fence around this tree
Starvation would force you to steal from me!
Here's another thing a monk won't do,
Go out at night and get on a stew,
Or use a gun, or a club, or a knife,
To take some other monkey's life.
Yes, man descended, the ornery cuss,
But, Brother, he didn't descend from us!"

*   *   *   *   *

Bigotry

We are God's chosen few. All others will be damned. There is no place in Heaven for you. We can't have Heaven crammed. (By Jonathan Swift, satirist)

*   *   *   *   *

A minister pulled this boner at a man's funeral: "Ladies and gentlemen," he said, pointing his finger at the casket, "this corpse was a member of the church for twenty years!"

*   *   *   *   *

An onion and a carrot went out for a walk on a very cold day. Mr. Onion did not notice how cold it was because he was a hot one. But his friend, Mr. Carrot, got so cold he finally fell down and couldn't go on.

So Mr. Onion called the emergency squad which took Mr. Carrot to the hospital. A doctor looked him over, and then talked with Mr. Onion. He said: "Mr. Carrot will be all right even after all that cold, but I'm telling you, he will always be a vegetable!"

*   *   *   *   *

Bishop Herbert Welch of the Methodist Church lived to be 105 years old. In 1972 his friends had a birthday party for him when he was 100 years of age. When he was asked for his words of wisdom, he said, "I have great consolation at passing 100 years. Few people die at 100 years of age!"

*   *   *   *   *

A fellow, not a Christian, wondered what all the excitement about Easter had to do with faith in God. So he stayed up all night before; then it *dawned* on him!

*   *   *   *   *

Peter Cartwright, the eccentric Methodist revivalist of the late eighteenth century, was a ready wit for almost any occasion. Once, when he rode in a town, some young men recognized him and decided to have some fun. As Peter tied up his horse to a hitching rail, one of the fellows came to him saying solemnly, "I suppose you have come back for the funeral."

"Whose funeral?" asked Cartwright.

"Why, haven't you heard? The devil is dead!"

"Is that so?" sadly remarked the old circuit rider.

Then he reached into his pocket, drew out a coin, and handed it to the spokesman.

"Why, what is this for?" came the question.

And then Peter said, "My religion has taught me to be kind to orphans!"

*   *   *   *   *

After an earthquake that shook things so badly many buildings were leveled, an old man was found in the rubble, sitting in a bath tub, stark naked. He was heard muttering, "I can't believe it! All I did was pull the plug!"

40

* * * * *

Coffee dunkers' plea:
> As you go through life, brother,
> Whatever be your goal;
> Keep your eye on the doughnut
> And not upon the hole."

* * * * *

Remember, credit cards are buy passes.

* * * * *

On communication:

I know that you believe you understand what you think I said; but I am not sure you realize that what you heard is not what I meant.

* * * * *

Little boy: Dad, did you go to Sunday School when you were a little boy?
Dad: Why certainly. I never missed a Sunday.
Little boy: Well, it won't do me any good either!

* * * * *

At another Sunday School, a teacher used an acorn to illustrate growth of faith. When finished, the Sunday School Superintendent arose to close the session and said, "We are thankful for the lesson from this nut."

* * * * *

One of the women's liberation advocates asked Bishop Kenneth Goodson, a United Methodist, "Do you still believe in a personal devil?"

He answered, "Yes, and she didn't like it!"

* * * * *

A visiting bishop delivered a speech at a banquet on the night of his arrival in a large city. Because he wanted to repeat some of his stories the next day, he requested reporters present to omit them from their accounts to the press.

A rookie reporter, commenting on the famous man's speech, finished his report with this line: "And the bishop told a number of stories that cannot be published."

26. The Tidal Bore

At Moncton, New Brunswick, Canada, one can witness this most unusual phenomenon: the tidal bore from the Atlantic Ocean.

At low tide there is just mud and a trickle of water in the bottom of the river. When the tide changes we behold a complete change of scenery. In a few moments the trickle backs up, followed by an inrush of ocean water. It gains crescendo even as one watches it, as it fills up the river banks and overflows onto the lowland flats nearby. What a tremendous display of energy, pressing onward and upward.

We feel the uplift of our spirits with the incoming tide.

Dr. E. Stanley Jones in his writings referred to the "tides of the Spirit" when God comes upon us with his refreshing Divine Presence. We need the spiritual tidal bore in our lives.

27. This Old House

Not all Senior Citizens are pessimists. Some are positive thinkers regardless of physical infirmities.

John Quincy Adams, sixth president of the United States of America, in his retirement was in conversation with a friend as they met on a Boston street.

"Well, how is John Quincy Adams today?" asked the friend.

Adams smiled and said, "Fine sir, fine! But this old tenement that John lives in is not so good. The underpinning is about to fall away. The thatch is all gone off the roof, and the windows are so dim John Quincy can hardly see out anymore. As a matter of fact, it wouldn't surprise me if before the winter's over he had to move out. But as for John Quincy Adams, he never was better ... never was better!"

What a marvelous expression of the real John Quincy Adams, not to be stopped by the "old house" he had inhabited.

Do you suppose this could have inspired the author of the popular song, "This Old House"?

28. Now Consider Seeds 3000 Years Old!

Scientists were given seeds discovered when tombs of ancient kings of Egypt were opened. These seeds had to be at least 3000 years old. Would the seeds grow? A test was performed to discover the answer to that question.

Some of the seeds were carefully placed at the right temperature and where they would get proper light. They were watered every day. The best soil was used in which they could grow.

In about three weeks something startling began to happen. Not only did the seeds swell up, but some actually began to grow into plants! Eventually, the plants were mature and grew seeds of their own. These turned out to be vegetable seeds much like a pea or lentil seed, and they were edible. The experiment was a great success.

Never give up if the seed you have has a purpose to live. Age of the seed seems to have been unimportant. Its purpose can be most important.

29. Take Me To The Cross, And I Can Find My Way Home

A little boy stood crying at a busy street intersection. When he was asked why, he said he was lost. Yes, he knew his name but not his home address.

Upon further questioning of landmarks near his home, the church was mentioned. The boy brightened up and said, "There's a church with a cross that's lighted at night near my home." He thought a bit, then said, "Take me to the cross and I can find my way home."

Out of the mouths of babes comes wisdom!

(A popular religious song has been produced on this theme.)

30. Pollution — What Really Is It?

Modern civilization is bugged by the problem of what to do with rapidly accumulating trash and garbage. The litterbug has ruined the beauty of some of our national parks; and our highways constantly have to be cleaned due to the thoughtless behavior of motorists.

As for the air we breathe, smog causes respiratory illness in big cities. The water supply must be guarded from contamination. Food and medicine must not be polluted either. Especially provoking is knowing what to do with atomic waste products.

It is all a material parallel to the spiritual pollution we call *sin*.

Not only that, material pollution often has moral implications as well. Our earthly environment is seriously involved in the effect it has on all areas of human lives.

44

Even as we must stop material pollution, we need the redeeming grace of God to stop our spiritual destruction by sin and evil.

31. Why Should I Worship A Dead Jew?

A young Jewish man started attending some evangelistic services held by the Reverend Alfred Henry Ackley. After five or six nights he waited to talk with the minister after the service. This was his question: "Why should I worship a dead Jew?"

This question startled Brother Ackley, whose forthright emphatic answer was, "He lives!"

After his re-reading of the resurrection story in the Bible, the words "He is risen" struck Ackley with new meaning. As a result, he sat down at the piano. The thought of God's ever-living presence brought to him the music promptly and easily for the convincing song, "He Lives!"

(From *Forty Gospel Hymn Stories*, Rodeheaver-Hall Mack Co., Winona Lake, Indiana.)

32. Balaam And His Talking Donkey

This story, in the midst of some rather dull reading in the Book of Numbers (Chapter 22:20-35), is a striking illustration of how difficult it is for mankind to see the truth when he does not want to accept it.

Balaam, a hireling prophet, set out to prophesy just what Balak, the king of Moab, wanted him to say against Israel. En route he was aggravated when his animal turned off the road into a field, so Balaam beat the animal. They moved on to a narrow place in the road and the donkey tried again to turn off the way and crushed Balaam's foot against a wall. He beat the animal again.

Finally, they came to a place where the donkey just laid down in the road and refused to move. As Balaam was beating the animal it spoke to him. Remarkable! The creature indicated it had always done his will before but this time it could not do so.

Then it was that Balaam saw for the first time the angel of the Lord blocking the road. It took a beast of burden to make this stubborn prophet realize that God was the reason for the unusual actions.

Balaam was not the only person to have his way blocked by God in an unusual event. Paul, on his way to Damascus to persecute the Christians, also met God in a striking event that blinded him physically so he could see spiritually.

Must God speak again through animals, or by some other unusual event, to get us to comprehend his eternal truth for our age?

33. From War To Peace

We go to a concert hall and listen to the sounds of different musical instruments as they tune up for the concert. Clashing of sound comes from the booming bass horn, with the shrill notes of a violin E string; and there is the rumble of drums against the wistful tones of a French horn. They are all going at the same time.

But then the conductor of the Philharmonic arrives. The noise ends when he steps to the podium and calls for attention. He is the master of the moment. He commands, and they act according to his will. Beautiful music comes as the conductor directs them in a fine program. Where once chaos of sound existed, now there is organized music.

On September 2, 1945, at the Japanese surrender to end World War II, aboard the *USS Missouri*, General Douglas MacArthur spoke prophetically:

> "*If we will not devise some greater and more equitable system, Armageddon will be at our door. The problem basically is theological and involves a spiritual recrudescence (revival) and improvement of human character that will synchronize with our almost matchless advances ... of the past 2000 years.*"

When will the time come that humankind will change the chaos of this world to something beautiful by submitting to their Master, Jesus Christ?

34. Something That Doesn't Like A Wall

An outstanding Christian layman, Branch Rickey, once owned a major league baseball team. He called into his office a baseball player, Jackie Robinson, and offered him a most unusual proposition, the first of its kind in major league baseball. Would Jackie be the first African American major league ball player?

Until then there were no African American baseball players in the major leagues. After much discussion, during which they faced the realities of the offer, Jackie consented to do it.

There was much criticism proclaimed when the deal was announced publicly. And when Jackie went out on the diamonds in those first games he played, he was insulted, ridiculed, and laughed at out loud.

Mr. Rickey also received criticism. "It won't work," the critics said. But it *did* work!

Jackie proved to be an excellent ball player who could keep his cool amid the hubbub. Time has shown that the racial wall could come down, and today baseball is an integrated sport. In fact, the idea spread to other forms of athletics as well.

Doesn't this speak a vital word to the continued plague of racism in other arenas of society?

35. Use What You Have

It is a striking fact that God has different ideas from us on how to accomplish a difficult task. We usually will say, "It can't be done," or, "We are not trained for that," or some other excuse.

When God told Moses what he wanted him to do — go to Egypt and make Pharaoh set free the children of Israel — Moses made excuses not to go, as we do. After several excuses were given, God used a shepherd's rod to teach Moses a vital lesson.

When serving God, use what you have!

For Moses it meant his right hand stretched forth. From his hand his rod dropped before Pharaoh became a snake. When he stretched forth his hand toward the Red Sea, the waters receded so that all of the Israelites could go across on dry land to the other side. Moses again stretched his hand back over the sea and the waters closed in over the Egyptian army. Moses used what he had and God blessed it.

Some of us can sing; others can teach; another can make things of wood or stone. We all have something, or can do something, for the Lord. God will bless us if we use what we have to his glory.

36. Something Better

In the movie *Green Pastures*, there were heavenly scenes portrayed as described by an illiterate black pastor. People were floating around on clouds, and there was a perpetual fish fry for everyone. It was the old pastor's version shown in a humorous way. God appeared to be dressed like a prominent businessman.

There was one scene never to be forgotten where Moses was high on a mountain east of the Jordan River, watching the children of Israel prepare to move into the Promised Land. Moses could not go with them, and he was very sad.

The Lawd (as he was known to the pastor) came to him, and they talked about it. "No," said the Lawd, "I couldn't let you go with them and you know why, because you were disobedient." Moses looked down dejectedly.

The Lawd went on. "Moses, you have been a good man. You led my people for forty years in the wilderness so they could go into the Promised Land. Moses, come with me: I've got something else for you. Something better!"

The Bible says no one knows where Moses was buried. He died on that mountain. But the Lord had something better for him. What else, but Heaven!

37. He Got Our Men To Singing

In the 1970s a likeable person to know in Circleville, Ohio, was the chief radio announcer for WNRE, AM and FM. He played the piano on the air in a folksy manner. His Irish name was P. J. Ryal.

Soon after our arrival in the town we met "P. J." in the grocery store of a mutual friend, Mr. Ward Skinner. P. J. began attending our church with his family.

Then one day Mr. Skinner said to me, "I think P. J. is ready to make a commitment to Christ and our church." Mr. Skinner was lay leader of Good Shepherd United Methodist Church, and when I suggested he might go ahead with the man he answered, "He wants the pastor to talk with him about it."

So on a Saturday morning in May 1980, when his wife said P. J. would be at home, I made a house call. We sat at the kitchen table and shared coffee. I told him why I had come.

"Two things I am asking of you, P. J. First, I ask you to make your commitment to Jesus Christ as personal Savior. And second, I'd like for you to get our men of the church to singing gospel music."

He thought a bit, then put his fist down on the table and said, "I'll do it!" And believe me, he did! He and his wife joined our church and I baptized their first child.

But even more, he came to our Saturday morning men's prayer breakfasts at church, then he would get the men around him at a piano and they practiced singing songs like "What A Friend We Have In Jesus," "Mansion Over The Hilltop," "I'll Fly Away," "Amazing Grace," and "Turn Your Radio On," and "Listen To God's Radio." The men loved it. Breakfast attendance increased from six to ten present, to twenty to 25 present.

They began to sing in morning worship one Sunday a month. It was well-liked, not only in the sanctuary but also by the listening radio audience. Our Sunday morning worship services were on the air every Sunday on WNRE from 9:30 to 10:30 a.m..

The contagious spirit of P. J. Ryal captured the spirits of men who mostly sang the melody; some of them did not read music notes. But they sang enthusiastically in community gatherings also, and even for the United Methodist District Conference one year. Oh, the power of sincere commitment!

38. Children Playing "Automobile"

Before television, when children had to be creative in their play, some children decided to play "automobile." There were at least twelve who had become tired of the usual ball games, etc.

So they decided who would be the headlights, who would be the motor, who would be the steering wheel, who would be the tires, and who would be the spark plugs. Then they started down the street. The child who was to be the horn made a tooting sound.

A man asked them what they were doing. They told him, "We are playing automobile." They each told what part they represented.

Then the man asked the two smaller children who stayed behind, "What part are you?"

They answered, "We are the *smoke* and the *smell!*"

39. The County Extension Agent — He's For Change

Because of our years in the ministry in town and rural communities we became well acquainted with the work of the Ohio State University County Extension Services.

All counties had at least an agricultural agent, and some had also a home services agent and possibly a youth agent. These agents were all committed to assisting people in making life better, not only in agriculture but also in home making and in the 4-H club work with youth.

One of these fine people described his work as a "change agent," since he was giving rural people advice for improvement in their farm operations.

I thought how ministers of the gospel are also "change agents" seeking to show people a better way of life.

40. Streams In The Desert

Not only did Isaiah give us a beautiful metaphor of how God's Kingdom can flourish in the desert place of life (Isaiah 35:6), but the phrase "streams in the desert" is the title of a best selling book. How it came to be written is a striking illustration that will encourage any believer.

Dr. Charles Cowman was a veteran missionary in China, an authority on China and the Far East. He was the founder of the Oriental Missionary Society, now known as "OMS International." Dr. Cowman became seriously ill and lay dying of cancer for six years. Lettie, his wife, stayed by his side through it all.

How does one deal with pain so severe he cannot sleep? Dr. and Mrs. Cowman found a way worth knowing if we are faced with similar circumstances.

Psychologically, we cannot deal with two subjects at the same time. We must keep our mind occupied with a positive subject, and thus avoid letting the pain dominate us.

The Cowmans had a map of the world placed on the wall beside the bed of Charles. They would divert thoughts and prayers to a country or a large city of the world, and pray for the people in those places. Their wide acquaintance with many missionaries of other societies besides their own gave them many names for their list. Appropriate Bible passages dealing with the people, and especially those portions that give help and vision to the suffering, were studied. Lettie recorded their thoughts.

Sometimes a poem or hymn would come to mind and this was also recorded. Quotations from other inspirational writings were included. After the death of Dr. Cowman, his wife made up a book from these materials, titled *Streams in the Desert* (Zondervan Publishing House, Grand Rapids, Michigan 49530). It was published in 1925.

This book has sold in the millions of copies, printed in over a dozen languages; its ministry is world-wide. Even as Isaiah 35 has been a blessing to millions of readers through hundreds of years, so this book has brought spiritual refreshment and words of encouragement to its readers.

41. God's Hitchhiker

A woman had prayed for her uncommitted husband and believed that God would some day reach the man's heart. But he died suddenly in a car accident, and the woman was so upset that she began to doubt God.

Later she learned that her husband had picked up a hitchhiker as he traveled along. In the conversation in that car, the hitchhiker succeeded in helping the husband commit his heart to Christ. Traveling on, the hitchhiker came to his destination and was dropped off, while the husband drove on and died in the car accident yet that day.

When the announcement was made on radio and television that this prominent citizen had died, the hitchhiker, after much time and effort, was able to contact the wife and inform her of that conversation, much to her surprise and joy. A coincidence? Hardly.

Don't ever doubt God's providence.

42. Handicapped Charlie

Our last dog was a Boston terrier named Charlie. Recovering from a cancer operation, I was not yet sure if I would or would not have cancer the rest of my life. Charlie came to our home because he was not wanted elsewhere. Out of a litter of four pups he had handicaps. Nature had dealt him a blow in giving him a cleft palate and a hare lip. Besides that, he limped when he walked.

But Charlie knew I wasn't so well off either. We took to each other right away. He'd crawl up in my big easy chair beside me and snuggle up against me trustfully. I still miss him.

Charlie never let on that he was handicapped, even though it slowed him down a bit. He had adapted his eating habits so most food was manageable with such a mouth. Charlie taught me a lesson:

> We are handicapped in spirit only as we allow ourselves to be. Physically we may not be able to change, but it doesn't have to destroy our spirit.

Some of the best spirited people I know or have heard about have handicapping conditions. A fellow seminary student years ago had an immobile arm and hand, but he typed his letters with the other hand and carried on a successful ministry. Joni Erikson Tada, though paralyzed from the neck down, has carried on an active ministry from a wheelchair and has had a fine radio program on many Christian stations in the USA.

43. The Friendship Bridge

What a blessing a bridge can be!

Years ago it was a problem to go from one side of the Detroit River to the other. On the West was a growing American city: Detroit, Michigan. On the East side was another growing city: Windsor,

53

Ontario, Canada. Ferry boats were unable to handle the volume of business created by the two cities.

Finally, a great bridge was proposed to span the river. Each side was to build on its own shore the necessary abutments, and then reach out to the middle of the span. Engineers drew up plans and supplies were obtained.

When the structure was started, it looked like a formidable task. Much hard work went into the construction. But as the spans reached out over the river below, interest began to grow. Week by week the arms reached toward each other, beckoning the workmen to come closer.

What a great day that must have been when the two spans were near enough the men could hear each other talking, high over the Detroit River. It was a time of rejoicing when they could proclaim the task of building "The Friendship Bridge" was completed.

Are we not supposed to be building bridges of friendship in various areas of life? And how about bridges for interpersonal relationships? You take it from there ...

44. From Pop Cans To Countryside YMCA

Ralph J. Stolle, the man who designed and patented the easy open soft drink cans now used by the millions in our land, grew up in Warren County, Ohio. He attended country schools and a country Methodist church where he learned lasting Christian values. He learned to share what he had. His inventions made him a multi-millionaire.

In his mature years, Mr. Stolle made possible a gift to his hometown community, a tremendous blessing to the Countryside YMCA. Located at the south edge of Lebanon, Ohio, this "Y" serves thousands of people coming from 35 to 40 miles in all directions. It is considered one of the largest and best equipped YMCA buildings in the Midwest.

Family oriented, there is something at Countryside "Y" for people of all ages, from nursery children with pacifiers in their mouths to Senior Citizens in their eighties and nineties. An excellent staff of 26 people serve those who come daily. Rates to join are quite reasonable. There is a complete schedule of all forms of indoor and outdoor athletics, with various kinds of exercise equipment. The Senior Center alone cost over two million dollars, offering special programs such as Aquatic Aerobics using a heated swimming pool.

What a striking gift, and to honor Jesus Christ! One of the staff has said, "The name of Jesus Christ is not a swear-word at Countryside Y."

Their mission statement includes: "We seek to develop Christian personalities through the improvement of the physical, mental, social, moral, and religious conditions of all who are served here."

45. The Laser Beam

It is so fantastic what the laser beam has done for mankind. Not only has it changed from a scattering brilliance of the usual bulbs and lamps, but it has resulted in a powerful concentration never before known in the world.

The laser is used as a sophisticated tool in intricate surgery on such subjects as the human eye. New uses are being found almost daily by modern industry.

This should be a striking suggestion to us that we should concentrate on using our human energies in such ways that God will be assisted in redeeming the world. New ways of taking the gospel to every nation are needed. It is amazing what a dedicated mind can come up with for the good of everyone.

The noted evangelist, Dwight L. Moody, once said, "The world has yet to see a man completely dedicated to God." Saint Paul, like a spiritual laser beam, was an example of such pioneering leadership.

L - ight
A - mplification by
S - timulated   Very high concentration
E - mission of
R - adiation

46. See You Later

The age-old expression "Good-Bye" seems to have fallen by the wayside. It really was a coined word: a shortened version of "God-be-with-you."

Even telephone conversations now often end with "Bye-Bye," or "So long," or "Be happy," or the popular "Have a nice day."

I prefer "See you later" for Christians. It is a fact, based on the Bible, that Christians never need to say "Good-Bye" as if they will never meet again. We believe that death does not end it all. Even in the glorious future we may meet again, "to know as we have been known" (1 Corinthians 13:12 KJV).

What a great thing it is to say, "See you later!"

47. Give Me This Mountain

Only two men, over twenty years of age, outlived the long forty years of the Israelites wandering in the deserts between Egypt and the promised land: Joshua and Caleb (Numbers 14:26-30, 38).

They had been the only two spies (scouts) who believed that the Israelites could take the land God had promised them.

We read about the later life of Caleb, after the fine old scout was then 85 years of age. He gave a wonderful testimony of how God had given him strength, from those days at Kadesh-barnea 45 years before, until this time of partitioning the land. His request was most unusual: "Give me this mountain!"

Joshua blessed him and assigned him his request, which included Hebron, because Caleb felt capable of this task before him and was following the will of the Lord God of Israel.

48. Crackers And Cheese

An old story often told but without much application was the one about a poor immigrant coming to America. He had saved barely enough extra to take along some crackers and cheese.

After most of the trip was over he became acquainted with another traveler. The poor man admitted to the other that he was quite hungry trying to get by on such meager fare. To his great surprise the other traveler informed him that when he paid for the trip, meals three times a day were included in the price!

The striking fact was that he was not aware of all the benefits of being on the way to his destination.

How many believe in Christ but are not fully aware of all the benefits along life's way? Not only are we assured of salvation and the eventual destination of eternal life, but there are many gifts God has for us along the path. The gift of the Holy Spirit to be in us and to guide us is the greatest of them all. He wants us to have more than "crackers and cheese," but to remember that Psalm 103:2 promises, "Bless the Lord, O my soul, and forget not all his benefits." Read also verses 3, 4, and 5.

49. Sleeping Through A Revolution

It was startling news to Rip Van Winkle to find out he was awakening to a new era in American life.

He had drunk too much that night before. It seemed so long ago. Why, of course, it *was* long ago. Many years had passed. Before that fateful night Rip was living in a New England colony that constantly spoke of King George of England as the tyrant who exacted taxes on them.

As Rip Van Winkle moved about in the colony he was hearing about another "George." Who was he? He was George Washington, the first President of the U.S.A.

Rip Van Winkle had slept through the Revolutionary War!

Washington Irving's story was not just a fairy tale after all.

With all of the startling news of our day, how many have slept through the revolution of *our* times? Read Acts 20:9-12.

50. The King Is Coming

When Jimmy Carter was President of the United States, he decided to spend a full day and night in several communities across the country. A certain typical country town in Iowa was chosen for one of those days, and the date was announced.

A decided change came over the town. Merchants fixed their store fronts to be more attractive; a lot of paint was used to give a fresh look to things. Even the people at their homes cleaned up, inside and out.

"The President is coming!" they would say. "We want things to be up-to-date and appear real nice when he arrives." It is quite stimulating to an average town to have the President come visiting. And he *did* come.

The Old Testament prophets foretold the coming of the Messiah hundreds of years before Jesus Christ was born in Bethlehem. The King was coming to his people. Why did so many miss him?

And would our society do any better today?

51. But Communism Failed ...

As the historic events took place, leading to World War II, serious questions were in the minds of thinking persons in Germany. Not only Christians like Martin Niemoller and Detrick Bonhoeffer, but Jewish people also.

One of those persons was the famous scientist, Albert Einstein, a Jew. He finally came to America and taught Physics at Princeton University. When interviewed, he told the questioners how he had watched the opposition to Hitler and Nasizm fall by the wayside.

He said editors of leading newspapers either became silent or feared death if they expressed any opposition in their news columns. He saw that the great universities which used to debate all sides of a question fell silent also. Only one force dared to oppose Hitler. That was Christianity, led by the courageous Martin Niemoller. The churches were opposed to persecution of the Jews, and to the concept of white supremacy.

So Einstein had to make a choice: either go to Russia and godless Communism, or to America where one is allowed freedom to worship God according to the dictates of one's own conscience. He chose to come to America.

Think of it! What if this Jew, the most brilliant scientist of his time, had chosen to go to Russia! Who might have had the first atomic bomb? Today we have lived to see the failure of Communism. Think about it!

52. The Towel Company

In Neil B. Wiseman's book *Growing Your Soul*, he suggests we all should become members of "The Towel Company," simply by doing something for someone else in the name of Jesus.

The twelve disciples of Jesus were taught this great lesson as it is recorded in John 13, when Jesus, their Master, laid aside his garments, took a towel and a basin of water, and began to wash their feet. It was an act of great humility.

What a sight that must have been! The immediate effect was voiced by Simon Peter who objected to it. Not that their feet were clean: they certainly were not. Nor were their hearts clean either, for one of them was planning to betray Jesus to his enemies. Peter did not think his Master should have to do such a menial task.

Jesus told him what true greatness was all about.

"The servant is not greater than his lord, neither he that is sent greater than he that sent him."

Must God teach his people again to be humbled?

We should all join "The Towel Company."

53. The Charred Cross Of Coventry

One of the most bombed cities of England during World War II was Coventry. The Nazis thought that they could break the spirit of the people if they bombed churches as well as factories. This they did with vengeance.

After the fire burned out at the cathedral in Coventry, the people attempted to clean up the place. While doing so, they uncovered charred timbers in the shape of the familiar Latin cross. They set it up in front of what was left of the sanctuary and held their Sunday worship services in that setting.

It became world famous. Rather than breaking the spirit of that congregation, it made them more determined than ever!

A new modern cathedral was built beside the broken walls of the old building which were still standing. Various chapels in the new Coventry Cathedral are centered on themes of today's society. But the most visited room was built in a circle with beams radiating from its center pointing to the ends of the earth. This room is known as *Chapel of Unity*, dedicated to human brotherhood.

When the new cathedral was opened, services were held with overflow crowds in every service every day for three weeks! It is still a worthy place for visitors to see and to participate in celebration.

But the central theme continues to be that old charred cross!

54. Who Was Mad Rhoda?

The Bible story begins with Simon Peter in prison for his preaching Christ, and some Christians gathered at the home of the mother of John Mark in a prayer meeting. No doubt they were praying for the release of Peter, who was heavily chained in prison.

That night an angel appeared in the prison, set Peter free from his chains, and led him to safety. He went to the house where the prayers were being offered on his behalf.

When a teenager named Rhoda answered the knock at the door, she saw him and left him standing outside while she reported to the prayer group that he was there.

"You are mad, Rhoda," someone said. But she was insistent, while Peter continued knocking, and finally they let him in.

How often has God answered some of our prayers in a miraculous way, and we thought the information was impossible. But God did answer their prayer. And Rhoda was not mad. (See Acts 12:13.)

55. The Compost Pile — A Miracle

What about the compost pile in the backyard? It's almost a secret.

Grass clippings, leaves, vegetables and fruit peelings, dried up flowers and garden plants, all go in it together. Add water and a small amount of agricultural lime and a miracle begins.

In a few months the decaying material has turned into a dark brown humus that can be used on flower beds and gardens to act as a perfect fertilizing agent.

Plants thrive in the enriched soil as we continue the recycling of what might have been discarded.

God takes our sinful acts, our leftover and burned-out spirits, and recycles them by his redeeming grace. What an awesome design he has for his universe, and also for our souls.

56. The First UFO

Some people think that UFOs are twentieth century phenomena, possible aliens invading our planet.

But if we read Ezekiel, Chapters 1 and 10, we could say he saw the first UFOs long before anyone else. What could such a sight mean to Ezekiel? If we can learn from his experience, it may help us to understand some of the unexplainable sights we may be seeing on our journey of faith.

One thing is to be impressed by our awesome God and his ways. What Ezekiel saw greatly impressed him. It really got his attention.

Another thing is the description of the commissioning of Ezekiel as a prophet in physical terms anyone could visualize. Such emotional events are hard to describe to others.

Whether it be Moses at a burning bush, or Ezekiel before fantastic living creatures, or Saint Paul blinded on the highway to Damascus, God will use whatever it takes to awaken leadership in our times.

57. Chance Or Providence?

Mrs. Claude Douglas of Los Angeles, California, had been downtown and started for home. She felt led to stop in a certain cafeteria for food. Looking for a table, she noticed a Japanese woman sitting alone. She went with her tray and joined the woman, and they were soon engaged in conversation.

Mrs. Douglas learned that the Japanese lady was on a mission from Japan to the United States.

Soon the lady took from her purse a card and said: "I have here a name of a woman in this city, given to me by my friend in Japan, who asked me to see her if possible. There is no street address and I have been unable to find anyone who knows her. Can you help me?"

Mrs. Douglas took the card and saw written there *her own name*! A chance meeting of these two women, in a city of 1.5 million people, is incredible. They must have been led to meet. It was Providence at work.

58. "God Owns My Business"

These words of Stanley Tam, Lima, Ohio, mystify some people. Stanley has a wonderful true story he has told of his stewardship in many churches and other places as a Christian witness.

When he was a struggling young man with a knack for salesmanship, he accepted Christ as his Savior and began tithing. He soon developed a business of reclaiming the silver from the plates used in photographic studios. Time passed and he prospered, so Mr. Tam was led of God to change his legal papers and make God his Senior Partner, giving 51 percent of his profits to the Lord's work.

Later, after branching out into the plastics business, Mr. Tam took a further step: he legally turned over *all* of his business to the Lord, and began working for a salary the same as other employees! The Stanita Foundation distributes sizeable amounts of money to various religious organizations, including more than twenty foreign missionaries.

Do they pay taxes? In 1969, for example, they sent over 300,000 dollars in taxes to the Internal Revenue Service from the profits of United States Plastics, and States Smelting and Refining Corporation.

Stanley Tam is a member of the Christian and Missionary Alliance Church in Lima, Ohio. He has served on the Board of the Oriental Missionary Society (now better known as OMS International). But he will tell you "God owns my business."

(From *God Owns My Business* by Stanley Tam; Word Publishers, Waco, Texas.)

59. Take My Silver And My Gold

She really meant it!

When Frances Ridley Havergal wrote those words for her famous hymn, "Take my life and let it be, consecrated Lord to Thee," she actually did pack up some fifty articles of jewelry, including a jewel cabinet she said was fit for a countess, and sent it all to the Church Missionary House of her denomination.

The hymn was written in 1874 and was not just poetry. She was born in Astley, England, daughter of The Reverend William H. Havergal, vicar of that city. She wrote other hymns and was a talented scholar, but with frail health. Death came at age 42.

Have you ever wondered if authors really mean what they write? To tell of such dedication in song means a lot more when we know that the writer meant it.

Frances said later, "I don't think I ever packed a box with such pleasure."

60. The Angel In Ebony

Ask any student or graduate of Taylor University in Indiana who Sammy Morris was, and you will hear the story of how God led this black boy in Africa from virtual slavery, to seek his goal of knowing more about the Holy Spirit by coming to America.

Born a tribal prince, he had been captured by another tribe and suffered severely, until one day Sammy ran away. He fled to a Christian mission where he heard the story of Jesus and accepted him as his Savior. Wanting to know more about God, Sammy traveled by faith to the Atlantic coast and worked his way across the ocean to New York City.

On the ship his living testimony of Christ was so compelling he led the captain and half of the crew to salvation. From that time on Sammy Morris was a soul winner.

His mentor in New York City was The Reverend Stephen Merritt, a leading Methodist minister and home secretary of Bishop

William Taylor. The pastor saw the tremendous possibilities in Sammy, and sent him to Taylor University in Fort Wayne, Indiana. Everywhere he went, souls were won for Christ.

The influence of this godly black student was far beyond anything the faculty or other students had ever witnessed. Truly, he was "An Angel in Ebony," as Stephen Merritt had described him.

The rigors of cold winter weather in the Midwestern United States was more than Sammy's frail body could stand. He had so earnestly planned to complete his studies and return as a missionary to Africa, but Sammy died in May of 1893. The impact of his death was so great that through the years hundreds of students have willingly taken Sammy's place and have gone forth to be missionaries for Jesus Christ!

61. You Are Not Home, Yet

Samuel Morrison, a missionary who served twenty years in Africa, was retiring and on his way home. Someone was supposed to meet him at the ship landing to transport him to his new home.

But the ship he was on also had President Theodore Roosevelt's party on board. Teddy had been to Africa on a hunting trip. He had bagged a black mane lion and other trophies. The Army Band, and what seemed to be half of New York City, had turned out to welcome the President home. Finally, after the President's party had gone, the missionary was at the ship's rail alone.

He looked up to Heaven, and said, "Lord, I do not understand this. The President was in Africa only one month and half the town turned out to welcome him home. I spent twenty years of my life serving you in Africa, and no one came to welcome me home."

All was quiet. Then it seemed to the missionary that the Lord answered, "Remember, you are not home, yet."

So, if life's struggles have gotten to you and you feel so alone, just keep trusting Him. Remember, you are not home, yet!

62. Daughter Of Independence

Probably no other emblem has had a more profound effect upon the American people than the Statue of Liberty in New York's harbor. What a tremendous sight it is! The first time one sees it the value of such a symbol is very impressive. To see it up close on Bedloe Island is even more awesome.

A gift from France to the United States of America, this splendid project began in 1865. It was hoped that it would be completed in 1876, the Centennial Year of our country. After numerous delays, the statue was finally erected and dedicated in 1886, with President Grover Cleveland as dedication speaker. Rebuilt 100 years later, this beautiful emblem stands to welcome travelers and immigrants to this country.

There are numerous stories of what effect the statue has had. Soldiers on ships returning from both World Wars I and II literally wept when they saw this "lady of freedom" representing what America means to all who see her. Emma Lazarus, watching immigrants come to see the mighty lady with a torch, wrote those oft-quoted words in her poem "The New Colossus":

> Give me your tired, your poor,
> Your huddled masses yearning to breathe free,
> The wretched refuse of your teeming shore.
> Send these, the homeless, tempest-tost to me,
> I lift my lamp beside the golden door.

Democracy is based on the assumption that liberty frees us from bondage. Ah, yes! But at what cost it comes!

63. Here I Am, Lord, Speak To Me

When God chooses to change the destiny of a nation he sometimes does it in a most unusual manner. He may begin with a baby boy, Moses, or later with a child, Samuel.

Samuel served as an acolyte in the temple at Shiloh, caring for the altar under the supervision of a nearly blind priest named Eli. His destiny was to become the first of many prophets of God in the kingdom of Israel.

In the night God called to Samuel. The lad misunderstood the call, thinking the prophet Eli needed him. Eli sent him back to his bed. But the same thing happened two more times, and Eli began to realize it was God calling. So he instructed Samuel to answer the call: "Speak, Lord, for thy servant heareth" (1 Samuel 3:9 KJV).

This was Samuel's sincere reply to God, who proceeded to give him his first instruction in prophecy.

How many more people has God called and they were not aware that God had something for them to do?

64. We Thought We Heard The Angels Sing

One of the miracle stories of World War II involved seven servicemen whose Flying Fortress plane went down into the Pacific Ocean and all but one of them survived after 21 days in three rubber rafts. With them was one civilian, Eddie Rickenbacker of Aviation's Hall of Fame.

All they had to eat was four oranges, the fish they caught, and a bird which had landed on Rickenbacker's head. They depended on rain water to drink.

Sergeant Johnny Bartek had his New Testament with him, which was a great blessing as they called on God in their desperation. Out on the huge Pacific they were so small and felt it keenly.

But God did help them; and afterward Johnny Bartek said that at one time "we thought we heard the angels sing." Mostly of nominal religious faith at first, maybe an atheist or two, they all came to know God in a personal way.

Another great epic of man's need met by a loving God.

65. What A Beautiful Pearl!

You know how irritation can upset a person. Sometimes a member of a church can drive a pastor to severe distraction. Every church seems to have at least one member who is such a menace.

It is a striking fact that we could learn a lesson from the lowly oyster. When a grain of sand gets into the oyster's shell, what does it do about it? The oyster begins to insulate itself by secreting a substance to cover the irritation. Then, with the movement of the water over the oyster bed the grain of sand begins to roll into a ball and eventually becomes a thing of beauty, a pearl.

In fact, persons with special training cultivate the development of pearls in oysters kept for this purpose.

Can we learn to insulate the irritations of life so that they no longer are problems but pearls? It is worth the effort to do so.

It's just an example of the redeeming grace of God.

66. It's A Myth!

A prominent citizen of a central Ohio community retired, and then spent a year visiting homes of citizens of the local school district to find out if it was true that school tax levies had been defeated by votes of Senior Citizens. This myth has often been stated by persons who just do not know the facts.

The study of the retired realtor revealed several things quite typical of many school districts.

1. There were not enough Senior Citizens able to vote to decide the issue. Health reasons prevented them from voting.

2. The persons voting against the taxes were other taxpayers, *many with children in the schools*, who were unwilling to add more to what they owed for their property, their new homes, and nice cars.

Hearing of the report from the study, a local factory executive reported that the company was considering moving operations elsewhere if the tax levies were not passed. They now have better schools!

This is a striking illustration of a myth that is like so many myths in our modern American society. It would be better to know the facts before placing the blame.

67. The Gates Of Hell Shall Not Prevail

It was recognition time for visitors at a service club dinner when the president of the club tried something different. The meeting was made up of members of various professions, and representatives of outstanding corporations of the community, plus a few visitors.

The president asked, "Will those whose company or organization you represent is now fifty years old stand up?" A fair number stood to be recognized, including some of the out-of-town persons.

Then the president asked, "If your company or organization has been around 100 years, remain standing." Some were seated while a few were still standing.

"How about 200 years?" the club president asked. Only a very few stood that test, so the president continued.

"How about more than 250 years?" One man, a visitor, remained standing.

"How old is your organization, over 500 years?" asked a surprised president. The club members were very interested. The man nodded in the affirmative.

"Tell us about your organization," came the request.

The man spoke, "I am the pastor of a church in another city of this state. You see," he said, "Jesus was the founder of the church and it has been around for over 1900 years and is still going strong!" (Matthew 16:18).

68. Twinkle, Twinkle, Little Star

A young boy living in New York City was reluctantly taking piano lessons. When it was announced that the famous Polish pianist, Paderewski was coming to town, the boy's mother thought if she took the lad to hear the great musician perform, it might stimulate his interest. So she bought the tickets and when the time came, they arrived at the music hall early.

As a typical little boy, he got restless, and finally got away from his mother by going to the men's rest room. On the way back to his seat he looked in a door and saw a vacant room, with a big grand piano in the middle. Curtains lined one side of the room. He went in the room, climbed up on the piano bench, and started to play the only tune he knew very well. It was "Twinkle, Twinkle, Little Star."

The stage hand had been told that when the music started he was to open the curtains. He did so, and to the amazement of the audience, and to the consternation of his mother, the boy was on the stage playing "Twinkle, Twinkle, Little Star."

Then an amazing thing happened. The great Paderewski came on stage behind the little boy, saying to him, "Keep playing, keep playing ..." He reached around the boy, and added marvelous music to the basic theme. No one ever heard it played like that before! When they were finished the little boy and the great Paderewski received a tremendous ovation.

Our Savior is like that: when we struggle, he puts his loving arms around us and says, "It's okay. Just try it again." We can call it the touch of the Master's Hand.

69. The Love Point Ferry

It was a trip never to be forgotten. After visiting some friends on the Eastern Shore of Maryland, we were returning to Baltimore, Maryland. Rather than drive clear up to the top of Chesapeake Bay and down the Western Shore to the city, we chose to travel by a ferry boat, from Love Point to a wharf at downtown Baltimore.

We left the Eastern Shore in late afternoon; dusk came on as we passed Fort McHenry, shaped like a six-pointed star. How would we know where to land, I wondered, as we approached a myriad of harbor lights. I went into the pilot's room and asked about it.

The pilot pointed to a special bright light, high up on a building owned by a wholesale tea and spice company. He answered my question by saying: "That special light above the harbor is my guide. I know that the landing wharf is directly below it. It will guide me home."

What light guides us home? Jesus, the Light of the World!

70. Redemption Is For Dedicated Buildings, Too!

In the 1950s, Graham Local School District came into being in rural Champaign County, Ohio. Named after A. B. Graham, founder of the 4-H Club movement, the consolidated school has been an excellent venture in rural education.

In the process, some buildings were eventually closed. One of them was the Concord Grade School building in Concord Township. A community meeting was held to consider what use could be made of the structure. Those present had attended the school there in their formative years, and they had a lot of personal interest in the building. What they have done with it is amazing.

Concord School building is now a lively community center. People of all ages are involved in activities there, from Senior Citizens down to children in athletics. There was a nice gymnasium-auditorium attached to the classrooms. The 4-H clubs meet there. They have fellowship dinners also.

The citizens themselves renovated the building which they found out had been well made to begin with. With some volunteer hard work the place is now quite attractive.

The striking fact is that the leaders of the Concord Community Center were youth in Concord Methodist Church in the 1950s. Today, these middle-agers are practicing some of the principles they learned in the church and public school years ago.

71. But If Not!

One of the striking stories in the Book of Daniel (Chapter 3:18) tells of three Hebrew men being cast into a fiery furnace. King Nebuchadnezzar, for a short period of history, was the most powerful man in the world. He had ordered those men to bow down to a huge golden idol, nearly 100 feet high, and to acknowledge the king himself as final authority.

The answer to the order by Shadrach, Meshach, and Abednego was courageous. They indicated they did not have to defend themselves, because their God was able to deliver them. They even went further to say: *"But if not, we still will not worship the golden idol set before us!"*

The Bible goes on to say God *did* protect them from any harm, and God was with *them* in their ordeal.

What a great demonstration of faith and courage!

72. Tragedy Redeemed

It was sheer tragedy!

James Timanus had trained, and graduated with honors, to be a medical doctor. He was then married, and with his new bride boarded an excursion ship at Detroit, Michigan, to celebrate with a trip on the Great Lakes before going to his medical practice.

But during the night the ship's boiler exploded and set a fire that spread so rapidly that many passengers lost their lives. It was the ship named the *SS Noronic*. Included in the lost were Dr. Timanus and his wife. Of course, the family back in Fostoria, Ohio, was devastated. What could they do now?

Insurance money from coverage for the excursion ship helped to redeem the consequences. The parents of the couple established a scholarship for pre-medical students at Jim's alma mater, The College of Wooster. Even today it provides help for physicians in the making. The goal of Jim Timanus is being met. Praise the Lord!

73. The Erector Set

The late United Methodist Bishop, F. Gerald Ensley, observed a boy building things with his Christmas toy, an erector set. The boy built a wagon first, then dismantled it completely and proceeded to use the same parts, plus a few more, to make a model airplane. The bishop told a denominational gathering how that procedure reminded him of God at work on individuals.

Here was a person quite needful of change. His whole being — body, mind, and soul — had been in serious trouble. But God was at work in the individual's life. He realized he needed a change in lifestyle and prayed about it.

God took his mind and renewed its processes. His body, which had been misused by bad habits and abused by drugs, was cleansed so that it could be used for a Christian lifestyle. God saved his soul.

Yes, he was the same man, but now he was a new being with better goals in life. The "wagon" had become an "airplane" to soar above his past way of life.

74. The Dead Sea Scrolls — What If ...?

The discovery of these famous manuscripts is universally known. A lesser known fact about them is supremely important. This is the story.

When the shepherd in the year A.D. 1947 found the scrolls in a cave near the Qumran Community by the Dead Sea in Israel, he had several options of where to take them for sale. It is not likely he knew the value of the contents of the clay pot, but he knew the pot would have value.

Of the various antique dealers he could have visited, he chose the shop of a Syrian Orthodox Christian named Kondo. Surely the Lord had a part in that choice! For Mr. Kondo was more than a antique collector, he was also a Bible scholar!

After the purchase, Mr. Kondo carefully opened the clay pot, saw what was in it, and contacted the Metropolitan (priest) of the

Syrian Orthodox Church in Jerusalem. Together they agreed to get another opinion, and that was when Dr. John Trevor from the United States was called in. Dr. Trevor was in the city attending the Center of Hebrew Biblical Studies on a study leave from Baldwin Wallace College in Ohio.

Dr. Trevor cabled Dr. William F. Albright at Johns Hopkins University, Baltimore, Maryland, about the discovery. Dr. Albright was the world's leading biblical archeologist at that time. He cabled back, "It is the most important discovery ever made in Old Testament manuscripts."

Suppose the shepherd had taken that clay pot to a *non*-Christian antique dealer!

75. It Takes Courage To Excel

On the wall of a gymnasium at Baldwin-Wallace College, Berea, Ohio, you may see this unusual sentence: "It takes courage to excel."

Why courage? Because it goes beyond the ordinary pattern of things, and anyone who seeks excellence will likely be criticized. It is much like the Christian who seeks to live a clean, holy life; he is often criticized.

But that is what God wants of us. Our world needs persons who will make the necessary effort to go beyond the ordinary.

When I needed cancer surgery I wanted the best surgeon I could find to work on me. My operation was a success because the surgeon excelled in his service to humankind. When I took flight by a jet plane to Europe I did not want a fairly good aviator as pilot, I wanted a pilot who was one of the best in his vocation.

It calls for the best for God's highest. He has done his part through Jesus Christ who excelled in his earthly ministry and sacrificial death. Can we do anything less?

76. The Christ Of The Indian Road

He had labored for eight years and felt like a failure. His health had failed, and he was broken in spirit as well as in body. It was a serious matter for E. Stanley Jones, Methodist missionary to India.

He had tried the usual approach of the times, post World War I, attacking weaknesses of other religions, using an appeal much like was used in Western society preaching a doomsday religion to the lost. The Eastern mind was not convinced.

A Brahmin gave Jones a clue to the right approach when he said, "I don't like the Christ of your creeds and your churches."

After much meditation and prayer two things happened:

1. God healed E. Stanley Jones completely, physically and spiritually, and assured him he would empower Jones in a better approach.

2. The better way God revealed to Jones was to teach *Christ*, not Christianity. The latter word was laden with overtones of Western civilization.

There would be no attack on anyone's religion. Christ would be placed in an Indian setting. Hence, the Christ of the Indian Road.

Did it work? It certainly did. Almost immediately, opportunities came to reach persons in the high castes of society, even persons in positions of national authority.

In the past, missionaries had primarily sought to reach the low, servant caste, and had found it hard to reach other levels of society in India. E. Stanley Jones became friend of, and teacher to, significant leaders like Mahatma Gandhi and Sadhu Sundar Singh.

Dr. Jones wrote a book about what is recorded here, and published it first in 1925. It became a best seller and for many years was required reading for candidates preparing for missionary service. The book's title was *The Christ Of The Indian Road*. Later, Dr. Jones wrote a sequel to it: *The Christ Of Every Road* in which he gave the underlying purpose of all Christian service.

77. Abe Lincoln's Serendipity

History records that before he was a lawyer, Abraham Lincoln was a general store keeper in Illinois. Trying as hard as he could, Lincoln just was not making a success of his business.

He wanted to be a lawyer, but preparation for such a vocation seemed almost beyond his reach. He would need to own and study important law books to be a lawyer. One such book was *Blackstone's Commentary On English Law.*

One afternoon a traveler came into his store needing provisions, but had no money. All the traveler had was an old barrel he would exchange for what he needed. Abe Lincoln realized the man's need, and he thought he might need a barrel some time, so Abe exchanged some food and fifty cents for the barrel.

After the man had gone his way, Lincoln looked into the barrel and saw among other stuff a book. He was amazed at what he had found: it was the very law book he needed, *Blackstone's Commentary On English Law!*

God moves in mysterious ways his wonders to perform!

78. By Faith Alone

It is a striking fact that when Martin Luther stood before the Council of the Roman Catholic Church, and was told he must recant his proclamation of "salvation by faith, alone," he never felt more alone in his life than at that very moment.

In his personal statement of that historic moment he said that he had no witness of God's Spirit then to confirm his faith. It was as if God had closed the door on him and he stood there alone.

But Luther was so convinced of his belief, based on the Holy Scripture, he dared to refuse the Council. It was not until later that night, after the Council had excommunicated him from the Roman Catholic Church, that he received *the witness of God's Spirit* in his soul that he had done the right thing. Time has vindicated his declaration of faith.

Saint Paul began the fifth chapter of his letter to the Romans with those powerful words: "Therefore being justified by faith, we have peace with God through our Lord Jesus Christ" (KJV).

79. Where Do You Think You Are?

A well-known gangster burglar died and in the next world found things to be very pleasant. He had all he ever wanted: a nice place to stay, plenty of good food and money, even had a car that was sleek and powerful. He also had a valet to assist him with his personal needs.

After a while he got bored with it all, and told the valet he missed those earthly escapades, like fleeing from the police after nearly being caught for holding up a bank.

"Would you like to do something like that again?" asked the valet.

"Oh sure," the burglar commented.

The valet told him it would be arranged. So it was that in this strange new world he was fully equipped, and actually did hold up a bank! It was all so smooth. It seemed like it was just too easy.

He told his valet it was thrilling, but it was just too good to be true. Then he said, "I thought Heaven would be different from this. Nothing ever goes wrong; I always win."

The valet answered, "Did you say Heaven? Sir, this is Hell!"

Who else may some day have a striking awakening that they are not in Heaven?

(Adapted from a radio and television broadcast on *The Twilight Zone*, by the late Rod Serling.)

80. Music And Warfare

Why do we have Army, Navy, and Air Force bands at our military establishments, other than for publicity purposes? Does music play a part in developing morale of our service men? Go to your Bible and read about King Jehoshaphat (1 Chronicles 20:21-29).

In the scriptures we read that this good and mighty king appointed musicians to go before the army of Judah, facing the Moabites and the Ammonites, praising God "for His mercy endures forever!" What an innovation that was!

Evidently praise and music to God has helped many others, if we read the Book of Psalms aright. Nothing demoralizes the forces of evil more than the inspiration that comes to the righteous as they go forth boldly praising eternal God.

So let the bands play on!

81. Masada

King Herod I of Israel was a fearful man. Because he feared reprisals against him by his enemies, he ordered fortresses to be built in his country. The most striking example was on top of Mount Masada off the western shore of the Dead Sea.

The leaders on top destroyed the ramp leading up the steep mountainside. The Roman army was taking over Israel step by step, and the last fortress to be taken was Masada. The year was A.D. 70.

When it became apparent to the mountaintop dwellers that they would soon be invaded, a leader named Eleazor called a meeting. There they planned how to destroy themselves in a systematic way. When the Romans did break through the final barricade they had a hollow victory. In the night, the people had met death by their own hands rather than be taken by their enemy. Out of more than 960 people only two older women and three children were found alive.

Such courage has been the basis for a rallying cry by every youth of Israel who will be trained to face enemies in adult life.

"Masada!" is that cry.

Shouting, "Masada!" by a native of Israel is akin to shouting, "Remember Pearl Harbor!" by an American.

82. The Love Of God

Years ago a mad man was reported to have written these words for a great hymn:

> *Could we with ink the ocean fill,*
> *And were the skies of parchment made,*
> *Were every stalk on earth a quill,*
> *And every man a scribe by trade;*
> *To write the love of God above*
> *Would drain the ocean dry,*
> *Nor could the scroll contain the whole*
> *Though stretched from sky to sky.*

Could any person, regardless of his sanity, have said it any better?

83. Gold For The King

When the wise men came from the East to see Jesus (Matthew 2:1), they brought lavish gifts for the new born King: gold, frankincense, and myrrh. One might wonder how such gifts could be used by the Holy Family. But time proved what each gift meant.

It would be expensive for Joseph to take his precious loved ones to Egypt, since King Herod wanted to destroy the child in Bethlehem who was the *new* King of the Jews. And it would take time for Joseph to find employment as a carpenter.

Gold — that surely was the answer! Provision had come in such an extraordinary way. When unusual events come in life, God will provide for his own.

84. Who Was Lost?

In the Bible story of Jesus at the age of twelve, several unusual things happened. Not only did he give evidence of his coming life's work, but what happened during the three days before Joseph and Mary found him was also significant.

After the feast of Passover, for which the Holy Family had come to Jerusalem had ended, evidently the group of travelers from Nazareth of which they were a part began the return to their Galilean homes. Joseph and Mary, thinking that Jesus was somewhere in the group, did not check on him until they had gone a day's journey. Jesus was not there. What consternation that aroused! Was Jesus lost?

They returned to Jerusalem, and after *three* days found Jesus, in the temple. The striking question arises, was Jesus lost?

The answer is no. Joseph and Mary left him right where he had been all that time. Jesus was never lost, but since that incident many have lost him out of their lives. Many are not aware that they are lost.

"There is a way which seemeth right unto a man, but the end thereof are the ways of death" (Proverbs 14:12).

85. The Titanic — "SOS"

When they were building this ship, it was to be the greatest ship ever to sail the seas! It had state-of-the-art equipment and was prepared to serve the finest food and entertainment available. It had been a colossal undertaking to build. Naturally the ship was completely filled with 2,223 passengers and crew for its maiden journey. The year was A.D. 1912.

But the mighty *Titanic* suffered a severe blow from an iceberg which caused it to start to sink during that night at sea. There were not enough life boats for all the passengers, when it became obvious the ship was going down. Panic reigned supreme! So sure had the builders been, little thought had been given to safety. A new invention, radio, might have helped that night, but the operator on the nearest ship was not on duty then.

Likewise, the mighty airship *Von Hindenberg* was seemingly invincible. After crossing the Atlantic Ocean it was destroyed by an explosion while trying to land at Lindenhurst, New Jersey. A striking fact about this was that its huge envelope could have been filled with non-explosive helium obtained from America. But those were the days when Germany and America were at odds with each other and those in charge of the airship did not think it would ever explode.

When will mankind ever learn? From the days of the tower of Babel to the time of the *Titanic*, man has often suffered from the delusion that he is mightier than God.

86. Old Faithful

The main attraction at Yellowstone National Park in Wyoming is a geyser shooting hot steam in the air. Amidst numerous other strange phenomena, this geyser, though not the only nor the largest geyser, is the most faithful of them all.

Day after day, year after year, there is an eruption approximately every hour. Hence the name Old Faithful.

Wouldn't it be nice if all Christians were just as faithful in serving the Lord?

87. They All Loved Wally

It was corn picking time, fall of the year, when the air was a bit frosty and a new leather jacket felt good. Wallace Stickley, a 41-year-old farmer, went to use his corn picker, with the intent of coming back to his house for lunch at noon. When he didn't come his wife went to see why not, and found him choked to death in a freak accident. The new jacket had caught in the machinery, bunched up around his neck, and he could not free himself.

When the news came, I went to the farm home to console the family and be of assistance as a pastor. I learned of the magnitude of fall farm work that needed to be done there. That night some farmers met at a local farm implement store and I met with them. Plans were made for a "Community Work Day for Wally." The ladies of our church then planned to have a carry-in dinner for all who worked at the Stickley farm that autumn day in 1954.

More than thirty farmers came with tools, tractors, and combines. They picked all of the corn that day, some soybeans were harvested, and fence was repaired, as well as completing other chores around the place.

We had an exchange student from Ohio State University at our home that weekend, a schoolmaster from Perth, Australia. He went with me to the Stickley farm and then to the wonderful church dinner at noon. When we met Mrs. Stickley that morning she had tears of gratitude for what those neighbors were doing.

"How can I ever repay them?" she asked.

"Those men loved Wally," I answered. "They ask no pay. They are doing the thing they can do best for you today. But we will share your appreciation at the dinner."

At noon, the men and the women who prepared the food responded with applause when we told them what Mrs. Stickley had said.

Our Australian visitor said, "I have learned a lesson here today that I will never forget. It was a lesson in brotherly love."

88. Dustpan

In Africa, in a missionary's house, a native boy was helping clean the floors of dust and dirt.

When the missionary brought out a dustpan in which to collect the dirt which had accumulated, the native African asked for the name of the dustpan.

The missionary had taught the boy how Jesus can save our souls and make us clean within. Then she told him the name of the object was "dustpan."

The boy asked, "Will you call me Dustpan from now on?"

What a sign of humble servanthood!

89. Small Things Are Important

On a wintry day we stopped at Ash Cave State Park in Hocking County, Ohio, to see an annual ice formation. Walking about a quarter of a mile we came to the largest open air cave in the Midwest. Before us was a huge icicle hanging down from the cliff above, almost touching the floor below. We went up closer to see and touch it, and it was wet. This icicle had been formed by one drop of water at a time from above. A small thing, one drop at a time, but look at what resulted!

Don't be deceived by the size of something; how important it can become. Two Presidents of the United States, John Quincy Adams and Rutherford B. Hayes, were each elected by a single vote. And in the 1960 presidential election only 63.8 percent of voting-age Americans went to the election polls where they elected the youngest person ever to serve the office of President of the United States of America by less than *one vote* per precinct. He was President John F. Kennedy.

By *one vote* California, Idaho, Oregon, Washington, and Texas became states of this nation.

One of the most important words we use daily has only two letters: *if*. Count how many times it appears in the eighth chapter of the Book of Romans in the Bible. This small word implies how conditional important matters can be.

90. Great Is Thy Faithfulness

This hymn is used widely in American churches. How many persons know the Scriptural setting for this hymn?

Jeremiah, the weeping prophet, sees for himself the desolation and humiliation of a once powerful city, Jerusalem. In spite of all his sincere prophecies and strong effort before the Kings of Israel — Josiah, Jehoaikim, Jehoaichin, and Zedekiah — the fact remained that he was ignored and rebuffed, and even accused of treason as the nation was taken into captivity. The great city of Jerusalem was pillaged and burned.

But listen to the lament of Jeremiah which gives us hope: *"It is of the Lord's mercies that we are not consumed, because His compassions fail not. They are new every morning: great is Thy faithfulness"* (Lamentations 3:22-23 KJV).

The hymn writer picked up the theme as he gave inspiration and hope that we also may realize that God will not fail us. Great is his faithfulness to us.

It becomes a striking message to our world with its wars upon wars: God is our only hope.

91. Stille Nacht, Heilige Nacht

It was just before World War II. Dusk had fallen, and Christmas Eve begun. The Princeton University campus was white with snow as carolers strolled from house to house of faculty members. They would sing a Christmas carol or two at each place.

When they came to a certain house they paused. Should they sing to a Jew? But in a festive mood they stepped up to the door and began to sing a carol. Soon a man came to the door and greeted them warmly. Then reaching behind him he came up with a violin.

Standing at the door he played while they sang such carols as "Joy To The World" and finally "Silent Night." Then he bid them good night with God's blessing and closed the door. The carolers were impressed and never forgot their experience.

The Jew was Albert Einstein, who had recently come from German. But after all, Jesus was a Jew ...

92. Lindy Did It!

In May 1927, the primitive radios and the newspapers came alive with news that where others with more sophisticated equipment and planes had failed, Charles A. Lindbergh (Lindy) had succeeded in flying non-stop from New York to Paris. Some reporters had called him a "dark horse" and a "flying fool" for attempting such a feat!

Some well-known aviators had tried and failed — Richard E. Byrd, Noel Davis, a man named Chamberlain, and a Frenchman, Charles Nungesser. One after another had problems getting into the air. Nungesser completely disappeared after his flight began; no one knows what happened. But Lindy was not discouraged.

He had taken with him a little food, a little water, a rubber raft, flares — and lots of fuel! A radio he thought was unnecessary weight so he left it behind. He was sleepy at times and said he flew by instinct and not by skill. He landed after being officially in the air 33 hours, 29 minutes and 30 seconds.

Later, with his wife Anne, they mapped out the Great Circle Route he had followed on his non-stop trip. (It is often called the "Lindbergh Route.") To this day it is a favorite route used by transatlantic flyers. They say you can't improve on it. It is just right! It could be done! Lindy did it!

93. Goodwill Industries

Elmer E. Helmes had graduated from Boston University School of Theology in A.D. 1905 when an economic depression changed his plans. So instead of being a foreign missionary he was appointed to a pastorate in Boston, Massachusetts. During his nine years at that church he saw a need to help people in dire poverty who did not want charity.

Pastor Helms went to a wholesale coffee house and obtained their used coffee shipping bags. He then distributed them to homes of wealthy Bostonians with whom he had become acquainted. Later he returned to pick up cast off clothing, and eventually also household goods. At first it was with a wheelbarrow, then with a horse and wagon, and finally with a truck. He hired the poor people he knew could clean and repair the goods. Gradually the work turned to helping the physically handicapped people he knew. They named the venture "Goodwill Industries."

By 1942 when E. E. Helms died, the program was already worth six million dollars a year. In 1970 in the State of Ohio alone, one million dollars was paid in wages to 2,400 handicapped people. Today it is the largest organization to use recycled goods benefitting poor and handicapped people in our country.

It is a striking example of how God redeems handicapped people as well as broken and repairable things.

94. The Rocks Cry Out

When early archeological explorations began a century ago in the Holy Land, there was some apprehension over it. What would they find out about Jericho in ages past? The Bible had been our one main source of information up to that time.

In fact, the Bible received severe criticism in the early years of the twentieth century. Various schools of thought arose and raised doubts about how authentic the Bible really could be.

Like taking an onion apart to find out what it is without learning anything, critics had dissected the Bible into documentary hypotheses, so much so as to confuse the average Bible student.

We now know this striking fact: There has never been any discovery in the rocks and other relics of the past that caused any reason to distrust God's written Word! It is amazing to learn that diggings around most of the important sites in the Holy Land, instead of changing what we know from the Bible, have all supported what was recorded centuries ago.

Literally the rocks themselves fulfilled the words of Jesus at that first Palm Sunday celebration recorded in Luke 19:40: "If these (celebrants) should hold their peace, the stones would immediately cry out."

95. The Power Of The Cross

We left after a Sunday morning worship service for the Columbus, Ohio, International Airport to start a trip around the world. Though I had removed my pastor's robe I forgot to remove the plain silver cross on a chain about my neck.

Seated beside me on the jet plane, an airline pilot for another airline greeted me as "Reverend" when he sat with us. I asked him how he knew I was an ordained minister and he pointed to the silver cross as identification. When he found out our plans he suggested I wear the cross all the time on our trip. This I did with striking effects.

The cross was observed more often overseas than in America. People would look at me and smile, and I knew what they meant. In one country a lady was unable to speak my language but she pointed to the cross, then to her heart, and nodded affirmatively. One man stepped up to me just to touch the cross and smile at me.

When we passed the border from India to Pakistan, the businessman in front of me had several parcels, two of which were confiscated: a bottle of whiskey and a box of cigars. I had nothing the inspectors could take but a good camera, so I was worried. But when the man saw the cross on a chain, he said, "Reverend, you and your family go right on through!" I was relieved obviously, and he was all smiles.

Oh, the power of the empty cross! We serve a living Lord Jesus.

96. The Light Of The World

While on a tour of Westminster Abbey in London, England, I turned a corner of a sun-lighted hallway, only to be confronted by a life-sized painting of a man standing before and knocking on a door.

I soon realized it was an original copy of the famous painting *The Light of the World* by Holman Hunt. Someone had added on a separate line at the bottom of the picture the quotation of Revelation 3:20 — "Behold, I stand at the door and knock."

Only eight original copies of this painting were produced by Mr. Hunt. None was placed more appropriately in any location than the one I saw that day in Westminster Abbey. As the sunlight poured in on that painting I agreed that Jesus *is* the Light of the World.

97. But In Spite Of ...

What a drastic sign of racism and hatred has been the burning of Black churches, predominantly in the southeastern sector of our beloved country but also in other areas across the land. There has been a serious feeling of futility in the hearts of members of those churches, as they realize that their sanctuary dedicated to God has been desecrated or destroyed.

But if those who set the fire think they have won a victory, they have another guess coming. It is a striking fact that these church fires have drawn together in common cause persons from all kinds of denominations and groups to stop the dreaded curse.

Such diverse organizations as the National Council of Churches of Christ in America, and the conservative Christian Coalition, are banded together to stop the violence. In spite of what has been done to violate or destroy sacred houses of worship, there has begun a strong ground swell to get a the root cause of such evil, and to stop it now.

May God add his continued blessing as new churches are built to replace those destroyed by such satanic forces.

98. I've Got A Glory

Archbald MacLeish, a noted traveler and author in years past, liked to tell this story:

It was in the heyday of the great paddlewheel steamboats on the Mississippi River. He had extra time on a trip, so he explored the boat from upper deck to the bottom hold. He remembered the sights and smells down around the boiler room. He was glad to go back upstairs on deck.

Years later Mr. MacLeish was traveling on the same steamboat. Again, he had extra time to explore the entire boat. But this time when he approached the boiler room he was aware of a transformation in the appearance of the place. It had been cleaned completely and even smelled better.

There was an old black engineer seated on a chair by the boiler. When the man looked up he had a twinkle in his eye when Mr. MacLeish told him he was very pleased by all the change.

The old man said, "I've got a glory!" His glory was to keep that boiler going and the room be kept clean.

Archbald MacLeish thought later about that statement explaining why the wonderful change. All the man had said was, "I've got a glory!"

Would to God that more people would have a "glory" in whatever their major responsibility in life might be.

99. Hurricane Andrew And Havoc

When Hurricane Andrew came to Florida to wreak havoc on the residents and buildings, the people had some idea of coming danger, so there was comparatively little physical damage to the people themselves.

But the property damage soared into the millions of dollars. It didn't take long to find out what buildings were built to stand such severe winds. There were some that remained standing afterward, but many of the homes had collapsed.

Now it could readily be seen why that happened. Many of them had been poorly built. Where there should have been more nails used to anchor the siding securely, only about half of the nails had been used. Structure after structure was so flimsy it was reduced to rubble.

We remember the Sermon on the Mount, Matthew 7:24-27, and its warning about poor building practices; and the words of Moses as he addressed the Israelites: "Be sure your sin will find you out" (Numbers 32:23).

100. Hymns And Gospel Songs

There is a striking difference between the stately hymns of the church used in the past hundreds of years, and some of the "gospel songs" born during the heyday of the Sunday School movement of the nineteenth century. Gospel choruses have come even more recently. Think of the contrast between the hymn, "A Might Fortress is Our God," and the gospel song, "Standing On The Promises."

A hymn celebrates the greatness of God with objective respect. A gospel song speaks of the subjective experiences of a believer, sometimes in lively testimony. Both have their place.

It was in 1874 that Philip Paul Bliss coined the phrase "gospel songs," having published a collection of such songs to be used in evangelistic campaigns, Sunday Schools, and youth ministries. He composed a number of such songs, including "Let The Lower Lights Be Burning" and "Wonderful Words Of Life."

Today we can use a variety of expressions of praise and song to the glory of God. (See Colossians 3:16.)

101. The Christ Of The Andes

The boundary line between the South American countries of Chile and Argentina had been in dispute for a long time. About a century ago the tension rose almost to warfare between the two nations. Guns were made and preparations started for battle. What could be done to stop it?

The Christian leaders of both countries were greatly concerned about it and made a special effort to avoid a lot of bloodshed, plus the huge burden of expense that could be the result. They went throughout their countries preaching and teaching peace and good-will. So much interest was aroused that the leading government officials took heed to their cry for a peaceful resolution. They finally settled the issue as to just where that border should be. There was no war.

The people of both Argentina and Chile were so pleased that they asked that some significant memorial be constructed to declare their peaceful intentions. Because of this there was built a tremendous monument high in the Andes Mountains on the newly established border. It was constructed using the metal of the cannon that were originally to have been used in warfare. It was formed into a huge figure of Christ the Redeemer, with his arms outreaching. It still stands today, a century later.

On a plaque at the base of the monument are these words: "Sooner shall these mountains turn to dust than the citizens of Argentina and Chile break the covenant for peace they have made together at the feet of Christ the Redeemer."

102. Lick The Pan

During childhood days Saturday was baking day at our house. Mother always had something special for Sunday dinner. Preparing for a cake, she would mix the ingredients in a big pan, then pour the mix into baking pans for the oven. I would ask, "Mom, can I lick the pan?"

She would say, "Yes." Then she would add, "But it will taste better tomorrow."

We here and now have the materials needed for a good taste in life. In many ways our generation has it better than anyone before us.

But "tomorrow will be better." Especially if it is with our Lord Jesus Christ in eternal life.

103. The Interstate Highway

Traveling over the Appalachian Mountains from east to west, we came upon a huge highway building project. Those were the days following World War II, when the Interstate Highway system was being built across the country. We stopped to read the sign at the beginning of that particular part of the system. It assured us that when this was completed travel would be far more convenient and safe through the mountains. They were literally moving away the side of a mountain!

We thought of Luke 3:4-5, a quotation from Isaiah's prophecy: "In the desert prepare the way for the Lord; make straight in the wilderness a highway for our God. Every valley shall be raised up, every mountain and hill made low; the rough ground shall become level, and the rugged places a plain" (NIV).

The Interstate System has been completed, but have we had a part in preparing that spiritual way for the Lord, which both Isaiah and John the Baptist prophesied must come?

104. The Drunkard And Easter

The phone call between Easter Sunrise Service and the regular Sunday morning service was from the police station. A man I had counseled for five months had broken his promise not to drink alcoholic beverages and had ended up in jail. He wanted me to see him. I took the time to go to the jail.

He was very repentant; he gave me his cigarettes, too. We prayed together that God would relieve him of his addictions.

I reminded him it was Easter, a time of new beginning for the risen Lord. It could be a time of new beginnings for him. I knew his wife would be a good supporter in his effort. So would I.

Here it is now, over thirty years since that Easter morning when that man did begin a new life. He has had no desire for alcoholic beverages since that Easter day.

105. When I've Gone The Last Mile Of The Way

One night I had a dream. It seemed I was in a fair-sized group of people who had gathered to wait for something to happen. No one was angry or seemed to be unhappy, so I guessed it was not a mass meeting to protest something.

There were some persons there who were distinctive in dress. One woman in pink was surrounded by some people, dear friends no doubt. A man I saw dressed in black was also surrounded by a group, and he was singing to them. It might have been Johnny Cash! But most of us were anonymous. I began to realize this was the end of something that had happened to us all. The mood was a time of celebration.

Then the woman in pink was gone! Vanished! And the man in black also! The people in groups were reverent in prayer: then they disbanded. What did it all mean? Was this the way life was to end for all of the rest of us?

I thought of Peter Jenkins who closed his popular book, *Walk Across America Volume II*, with a vivid description of how people he had met on his walk began to gather with Peter and his wife as they walked the last few miles of his journey to the Pacific Ocean. A song came to mind as Peter and a large number of friends finally went the last mile of the way. What a beautiful way to end a journey!

Peter has become a noted author and has written other books, so it was not the end of the way. What will it be like for us when we have walked the last mile of the way? You are invited to join a multitude of believers in anticipation of the future of God's love.

If I walk in the pathway of duty,
If I work till the close of the day;
I shall see the King in His beauty,
When I've gone the last mile of the way,

When I've gone the last mile of the way,
I will rest at the close of the day,
And I know there are joys that await me,
When I've gone the last mile of the way.